THE TALE OF

JULIET

Praise For *The Tale Of Juliet*

"Profound and compelling! The Tale Of Juliet is a transformational and inspiring account of doing whatever it takes to live life to its fullest potential. This book shows how to discover a higher purpose in life while enjoying the journey along the way."

T. Harv Eker

#1 N.Y. Times best selling author, *Secrets of the Millionaire Mind*

"A thoroughly inspiring book! Anyone who has risen from poverty will appreciate Jhet's story. Anyone who is still in poverty will take much encouragement from a woman who has been there and made such a tremendous life for herself."

Suzanne Anderson

Author, *Self Publishing in Canada*

"This captivating true story is a heart-warming reminder that we all create our lives through our choices and attitudes. When we combine determination and integrity, love and faith - we get the perfect recipe for success and fulfillment. Jhet's story inspires us to realize our highest human and spiritual potential despite change, challenge and adversity."

JoAnne L. Rush

Owner, *What a Rush Productions*

"Victor Hugo once said that the most powerful force in the universe is an idea whose time has come. In her book, The Tale Of Juliet, Jhet taps into this dynamic with the captivating events and activities in her life. A demonstration of admirable feat and leap of faith. Beyond doubt inspirational."

Fr. Stanley Galvon
Pastor, Good Shepherd Church, British Columbia, Canada

"Each page turned in The Tale Of Juliet conveys powerfully that Jhet is a woman who does it all at a pace few could keep up with. Her book is a success because of her spirit. She is not just a woman with a dream, she is living the dream! From her humble beginning, a spark to a flame, she now focuses on filling others with that burning passion to believe and achieve! This book is an inspiration to us all."

R. Brent Lang, CIM
Associate Portfolio Manager, Investment Advisor

"The Tale Of Juliet is a beautiful tapestry of words, woven by Jhet in such a way that you're hooked from the first sentence. Her story is a testament to an unrelenting and determined soul who candidly shares her faults, heartbreaks, lessons and triumphs. Don't miss this special journey with this special author."

Dahlynn McKowen
Co-author, *Chicken Soup's Soulful Guide* travel series

More Praise For *The Tale Of Juliet*

"Jhet is an angel sent from heaven above. Journey with her through The Tale Of Juliet as she rises against all odds from a poverty-stricken childhood to a life of abundance way beyond her wildest imaginings. This book is a magical story that will inspire people for generations to come with its gripping tale of faith, determination and courage."

James Lee Valentine
Founder, *The Empowered Millionaire Organization*

"Jhet's decision to write and share her story should serve as a spark to ignite anyone who dreams of writing their personal story to actually do it. Jhet helps us understand that everyone can make a difference and that there is no greater pleasure than making your contribution with meaning and passion."

Mark Startup
President & CEO, *Retail BC*

"This book will touch your heart and inspire your soul. It's a true testament of hope, courage, and determination and will inspire you to pursue your dreams!"

James Malinchak
Contributing Author, *Chicken Soup for the Soul*®

Sts. Peter & Paul Parish

5539 D. M. Rivera Street, Poblacion, Makati City, Metro Manila, Philippines

It is my honor and privilege to endorse this book of Jhet Torcelino-van Ruyven. Many years ago, her father approached me and asked if I could help his bright and good-natured daughter go to college. I did. Now, the young teenager has become not only a good wife and mother but also an outstanding leader. The secret of her success lies in her tenacity to actualize her dreams. She aspired to reach for the stars, and I think she accomplished it. Now, she wants to show her gratitude to the people who have shaped her character and her vision through her book.

Her life story will inspire millions of young people around the world but, most especially, in her own country, the Philippines, where teenagers constitute a huge percentage of the population. I hope and pray that her unwavering faith in God, which has sustained her through years of struggle, pain and success, will touch the minds and hearts of the young people of today and of the future.

MONSIGNOR ANTONIO B. UNSON, H.P.

Parish Priest, Sts. Peter & Paul Parish

"Living a life of gratitude, abundance and purpose."

THE TALE OF JULIET

YOU HAVE THE POWER
TO CHANGE YOUR LIFE

JHET TORCELINO-VAN RUYVEN

For information please contact:
For quantity discounts, corporate sales, bulk purchases and fundraising
Contact info@thetaleofjuliet.com or www.thetaleofjuliet.com

Library and Archives Canada Cataloguing in Publications

Torcelino-van Ruyven, Jhet -
The Tale of Juliet: You Have The Power To Change Your Life / Jhet
Torcelino-van Ruyven.

ISBN: 0-9738279-1-2

1. Torcelino-van Ruyven, Jhet-. 2. Businesswomen–
Canada–Biography. 3. Filipino Canadians–Biography. I. Title.

HC112.5.T67A3 2005   338.092   C2005-904047-5

Graphics, cover design and photographic layout by
Greg Bell, Katy Mayrs and Matt Poquiz of
Digi-Print Graphics Plus
digi-print@telus.net
Final critique and formatting by *Power Design*
design@power.ph

First Printing July 2005, Philippines
Published (2005) in Canada by
Digi-Print Graphics Plus
101 - 15585 24th Ave, Surrey, BC V4A 9Z1
digi-print@telus.net   www.digiprintgraphics.com
Printed in Canada

 # Dedication

The Tale of Juliet is first and foremost
dedicated to my parents, Tatay and Inay.
Tatay, this book is your dream come true
for your little girl named Juliet.
I will always be so very grateful for what
you have both been through for me.

To my beloved husband, Ted.
You are an integral part of this unbelievable journey.
Thank you for always being there for me.

To my darling daughters,
Michelle Christine and Catherine Maria.
You are the greatest miracles that ever came into my life.
This book is my legacy to you both. Always believe in your dreams.

To everyone who will come across this book.
You and you alone have the power to uplift your life.
Together we can make a positive difference.

And to all the wonderful people
who have in so many miraculous ways
enriched, touched and shaped my life.

I love you all.

Living a life of gratitude, abundance and purpose.

Contents

Part I

 Living a life of gratitude, abundance and purpose.

PART II

Living a life of gratitude, abundance and purpose.

Meet the Author

Jhet Torcelino-van Ruyven is an *enlightened warrior* at heart and an incurable optimist. Poverty was never a stumbling block to her as she pursued her dreams.

She started out in a tiny rural village in the Philippines where she walked miles and miles to go to school and earned a living as a peddler from the time she was merely seven. Jhet now is a world traveler having gone to Europe, Asia, Africa, United States and Canada.

Her unquenchable thirst for learning has brought her face-to-face with giant authors and speakers like Mark Victor Hansen, Robert G. Allen, T. Harv Eker, Nido Qubein, Jack Canfield, David Bach, Ken Blanchard and John Gray.

Jhet is the owner of Digi-Print Graphics Plus, a digital printing and graphics design company in South Surrey, British Columbia, Canada. She has a bachelor's degree in commercial science, with a major in management.

In 1996, she was nominated in Surrey as Business Woman of the Year. Despite having been broken into twice and having faced some legal challenges, she bounced back and her business continues to flourish.

 Living a life of gratitude, abundance and purpose.

Jhet is married to Ted van Ruyven, a Dutch gentleman, with whom she has two wonderful children, Michelle Christine and Catherine Maria.

Like the jet plane that skyrockets to the heavens with the burning of its fuel, Jhet's big dreams have propelled her to speed away and make them real against all the odds and fears.

The Tale Of Juliet is an incredible story of a woman who has conquered poverty, heartbreak and adversity. Your heart, mind and soul will surely be captivated by this powerful story book.

This tale is a fitting tribute to all overseas workers, immigrants and to humanity as a whole. Truly, a person fully alive like Jhet is God's glory.

Susan Romero-Vidal
Author of *The Gospel According To My Kitchen Sink*

 Living a life of gratitude, abundance and purpose.

Foreword

The first time I saw Jhet was at Mark Victor Hansen's *Mega Book Marketing University*. She was on stage with a group of people making short personal introductions. What struck me most about Jhet was her intense level of energy, which transcended her very being and made her appear larger than life — like an angel.

The next distinct character trait of Jhet, which hit me so forcibly and which marked her as a uniquely inspired individual, was the fact that while the rest of the group made totally forgettable speeches, Jhet didn't make a speech at all — she sang a song!

The words of that song still reverberate through my mind and are the epitome of Jhet and her rise against the most overwhelming challenges from a childhood of abject poverty to a life bursting with abundant riches.

The song that Jhet sang with so much passion that day was entitled *One Moment in Time*, the words of which are now embedded in my soul. Jhet's journey through life is a reflection of these words and her sheer determination to succeed is a mirror of her never-say-die attitude.

Journey now with Jhet on her heart-stirring tale of self-sacrifice and strength over adversity, as she transports you through time with her words of hope, courage and inspiration to all mankind.

 Living a life of gratitude, abundance and purpose.

Jhet takes you on a magic carpet ride from her humble beginnings in the Philippines, through her humilations, heartbreaks and trials, to her eventual successes all over the world. Experience the thrills as she triumphs against adversity to make her life's dreams come true, at the same time giving you, the reader, the desire to take action to positively transform your own life in a million miraculous ways.

Jhet is an angel sent from heaven above. Journey with her through *The Tale Of Juliet* as she rises against all odds from a poverty-stricken childhood to a life of abundance way beyond her wildest imaginings. This book is a magical story that will inspire people for generations to come with its gripping tale of faith, determination and courage.

God speed and happy reading!

JAMES LEE VALENTINE
Founder, *The Empowered Millionaire Organization*

THE TALE OF

JULIET

PART I

Living a life of gratitude, abundance and purpose.

 # CHAPTER I

TRIPLE INSPIRATION FOR *THE TALE OF JULIET*

"Jhet, you need to write a book.
You have a book within you!"
MARK VICTOR HANSEN

My name is Julieta Torcelino-van Ruyven. A nun-friend named Sister Eliza gave me my nickname *Jhet* — pronounced 'jet' as in jet plane. After you read my story, you'll understand why this name suits me perfectly. Most of my friends call me Jhet now — and you can, too, if you like. I was born in a tiny rural village in the Philippines called Pader (which means wall) in the province of Batangas. I am the third eldest in a brood of twelve children.

My family was very, very poor. At the tender age of seven, when most children are outside playing, I started my very first job. I helped my parents by selling fruits, vegetables and even candies — anything that would help eke out our family income. Take a moment to imagine a very petite, very brown, barefooted child with a *bilao* (woven container) on her head and a basket slung over her shoulder. Now imagine this little child walking for miles and miles in the heat of a near-equatorial sun or through fierce tropical rains, complete with thunder and lightning. That is how I was!

 Living a life of gratitude, abundance and purpose.

Life in rural Philippines was often difficult for our family, but that didn't prevent my parents from instilling in me the value of a good education. My parents were not able to realize their own dreams of higher education and they wanted a different life for their children. And so, my father and mother worked very hard to help provide for our large family. They wanted to feed and clothe us, of course, but they also had a burning desire to see us educated. Even though they were very busy trying to find ways to feed their young sons and daughters, my parents, more particularly my father, somehow made time to read to me once in awhile.

Our family didn't own any books, mainly because there were very few books available where we lived. There were no libraries where we were. Besides, the meager earnings of my parents were first and foremost allocated for buying food to feed our family. Money was hard to come by for them, and when they did have some income, the basic necessities like food came first.

It is good to note that when I was a child, we never seemed to lack for clothing, though what we wore was usually old and tattered *and* we often had no footwear. There was definitely no allowance for any books or any other educational materials. Instead, my parents would read to me over and over again the textbooks provided to us by the schools. My parents' patience, endurance and determination to give us a better life than what they had was a true inspiration to me, and the source of my fierce drive later in life.

Living a life of gratitude, abundance and purpose.

Come to think of it, I've always had inspirational people to help me along my journey. I like to call them the angels of my life. They are angels without wings, of course, yet their contributions are hugely important to my life's successes. It's amazing what happens when we pay attention to the opportunities presented to us in life. What I mean is, people come and go in our lives, but they all bring gifts, insights and hints about our higher purpose here on earth. When I look back, I can see Divine guidance clearly. Thinking about my father reading to me reminds me of many childhood moments that were distinctly providential. In fact, one of those moments is a manifestation of how this whole book writing adventure truly began.

THE *ALKANSYÁ*

It was my third birthday and my *Tatay* said that he had a little surprise for me. By the way, *Tatay* means father in Tagalog. In case you are wondering, Tagalog is the language we speak in the Philippines, not English, which we must learn as a second language. Anyway, on this special day, my *Tatay* called me to come to him and made me sit on his giant lap. Now, you must understand, my father is not a very big man, but he certainly seemed large to me at the time. I sat on his lap obediently and looked up to him with wide eyes. That was when I noticed the mysterious package in his hands. I watched with great anticipation as he slowly opened the puzzling parcel. He carefully removed the brown manila wrapping paper and to my great delight revealed a brand new book.

 Living a life of gratitude, abundance and purpose.

Books were very hard to come by where I lived, so to receive a brand new book as a gift was an extremely big deal. What's more, this was no ordinary book. This book had my name written on the cover. How incredible! You might be wondering how I could read my name at the age of three. I don't really have an answer for you. Maybe my father pointed it out to me or maybe I knew just enough to recognize and read my own name. Either way, I still vividly remember the size of the book — it was approximately eight inches high by five inches wide and quite thick — and the color was a graduated blue background with red rose-like flowers. Most of all, I remember what for me was the best part of that book, the words written across the front — *The Tale of Juliet.*

I couldn't wait to hear the story. I re-positioned myself comfortably on my father's lap, eagerly looking forward to hearing the tale. My excitement quickly faded. Instead of reading, my father simply remained silent and looked back at me with twinkling eyes. Extremely confused by his behavior, I decided to reach out and touch this book myself. I must admit I was a bit disappointed when I discovered that the book had no pages in it. In fact, it was completely solid! I wanted to know what was going on, and I wanted to know right away.

With a light-hearted smile, my father explained to me that this strange gift was not a real book after all, but an *alkansyá* or coin-bank. At that time, my father was working as a bus driver for a

 Living a life of gratitude, abundance and purpose.

company in Manila, the capital city of the Philippines. I later found out that he had a mechanic friend named Reyno who also worked for the same company and was the one who made the coin-bank. Apparently, Reyno offered to make one for my father so he'd have a gift for me on my birthday. Reyno asked my father what name he wanted on the coin-bank-book, and instead of a name, my father came up with a title, just like a real book — *The Tale of Juliet.*

My father explained how I could use the *alkansyá* as a savings bank for my future. As I watched in awe, he patiently described how to put the coins I saved into the little slot at the top and how they would stay safe until I was ready to use them. What a concept! My young mind began to reel with excitement. What possibilities did this little contraption hold for me? My earlier disappointment washed out quickly as I fantasized about having that little *alkansyá* full of money.

I can't emphasize enough how thrilled I felt seeing my name printed on the cover of this coin-bank-book. I felt really proud that I had a book named after me. I told everyone I knew. Whenever visitors would come to our *bahay kubo* (*nipa* hut), I would run and get the *alkansyá* and pretend that I was reading the story of Juliet to them. I must have appeared very clever because all of our guests (mostly relatives and friends from the rural village who had not seen anything like it) seemed so surprised when I revealed the secret to them that the book was actually a coin-bank.

 Living a life of gratitude, abundance and purpose.

A few decades later, when I was already a parent with children of my own, I realized my father had planted an extraordinary seed on that day when he gave me the *alkansyá*. It was a seed of hope and optimism, and the very beginning of understanding that I had the power to create my own future. Even though I was only three-years-old, to some degree I knew why the pages of that *alkansyá* book were solid. I knew it would be up to me to fill those pages with the stories of my life. It would be up to me to write and live the real *Tale of Juliet*.

Many years have passed since that special moment on my father's lap, and many coins have traveled in and out of the banks of my life. I'm not exactly sure what happened to the *alkansyá*. It stayed in our house for many years, reminding me to be proud, to dream and to look forward to a better and brighter future.

The amazing adventures that followed that day with my father will astound you. I have been transported through time from the beaches of the Philippines to the snowy peaks of Canada, from the oceans of the Caribbean to the jungles of Kenya. I've wheeled across Europe and whirled in California. Imagine, it all started with the tiny imaginings of a very small, very poor Filipino girl.

My friends, I am proud to tell you that the book you have in your hands right now is the real *Tale of Juliet*. It is a tale filled with down-to-earth experiences, laughter, hope, sorrows, hurdles,

 Living a life of gratitude, abundance and purpose.

triumphs and exultations. Mostly though, it is the tale of how I, Julieta 'Jhet' Torcelino-van Ruyven, created a life of gratitude, abundance and purpose. I invite you to listen to my tale. My burning desire is that you enjoy your time with me as you read this book and when we part ways, you'll feel a little more inspired to make your own dreamy tales a magnificent reality.

RUBBING SHOULDERS WITH A GIANT

Come with me as we fast forward to the year 2003. It was providential that I met and connected with Mark Victor Hansen. In case you didn't know, he is the very wealthy and very famous co-creator of the *Chicken Soup for the Soul* book series. Books in this series have been number one on the New York Times best-sellers list several times. There have been over one hundred million copies sold worldwide, in over thirty languages — mighty impressive.

I first saw Mark in Vancouver, Canada, the city my husband and I immigrated to together fifteen years earlier. Mark was in Vancouver speaking to the Retail Merchant Association. I am a member of that association so I decided to attend Mark's event. (Just so you'd know, whatever I do, I tend to do it with enormous enthusiasm, and this event was no different.)

Near the start of Mark's presentation, I somehow managed to make an impression on him. I was one of the very few participants

 Living a life of gratitude, abundance and purpose.

in the audience that he noticed and acknowledged from the stage. Did I mention that I am only four feet ten inches tall? Are you wondering how he picked little ol' me out of the large crowd? Well, as I remember it, he asked the audience if they were familiar with his *Chicken Soup for the Soul* book series. I really love that series!

My heart started pounding and I started waving my hand like crazy. I found myself yelling loudly that I had not only read the series but that I often gave away his books to friends and relatives. I think that he really appreciated my energy and sincere enthusiasm. He laughed and said that he would love to give me a copy of one of his books when he was finished with his session. It was a pretty exciting moment. Towards the end of his presentation, Mark kept his promise to me. After identifying where I was in the crowd, he actually tossed a copy of *Chicken Soup for the Canadian Soul* right to me, and I caught it! I felt blessed.

I really wanted Mark to sign that 'gift' book before I left, so as soon as he finished his speech, I hurriedly ran to the back of the hall trying to beat the rush of more than a thousand attendees. I maneuvered myself through the flood of people now lining up to invest in his inspirational books and audio programs. By the way, there are some distinct benefits to being small. I was able to squeeze myself through the people headed toward the front of the crowd. As I got closer, I noticed that he had only two people helping him process the hundreds of requested orders. My immediate instinct was to help. Instead of asking him to sign my book, I yelled over to him, "Mark, can I help? I have my own business and I know how to do this kind of work." I don't know if he remembered me from earlier, but to my amazement he replied excitedly, "I really like you. You're hired!" I didn't need any further encouragement. I leaped over the table and began the frenzied work immediately.

It was almost midnight when the bulk of the attendees left. Mark had completely sold out all his materials and only five of us remained. As we packed up supplies, we casually chatted, sharing our stories with one another. I told Mark about my very humble beginnings and how I was able to transform my life of poverty to one of abundance and wealth. That is when 'it' happened. Wow! I'll never forget the moment Mark Victor Hansen looked straight into my eyes and said, "Jhet, you need to write a book. You have a book within you."

I secretly wondered if this was a line he often used to motivate people. English is not my first language, so I shrugged my shoulders and laughed. I told him, "Mark, you do not know me. I do not trust my grammar." Still looking straight into my eyes, he said directly and emphatically, "Leave that to the professionals, Jhet. You ought to write a book." This time, I really heard him. After all, he was a famous author, wasn't he? He must know what he's talking about. I let his words sink into my soul that night and his powerful message awakened something deep in my heart. I suddenly

 Living a life of gratitude, abundance and purpose.

remembered the *alkansyá* my father gave me some four decades earlier. Was this a new prophetic sign? Was I supposed to write a real *Tale of Juliet* after all?

I saw Mark off to the escalator that evening, after finally getting his signature, of course. I bade him goodbye and made my way out to my car. I don't really remember how I got home that evening — home is a 45-minute drive. I think I must have floated home on cloud nine. I do remember that Mark's message "Jhet, you need to write a book. You have a book within you." rang repeatedly in my ears throughout my journey. As soon as I arrived home, I went straight to our kitchen table, sat down, and started dreaming. The entire night I sat there, just thinking about my life — the highs, the lows, the blessings and all the miraculous happenings that had conspired to bring me to this moment now. Before I knew it, dawn was breaking and I was very inspired.

A LITTLE FILIPINO INSPIRATION

About a year later (March 2004 to be exact), I traveled back to my old home in the Philippines, together with my husband and our two daughters, to celebrate my parents' 50th wedding anniversary. Their anniversary was actually in May, but my mother and father decided to have the celebrations early so that our children could make it. Their school's Spring Break fell in March, so we scheduled the main celebrations for that month.

 Living a life of gratitude, abundance and purpose.

When we were in the Philippines, my husband and I kept hearing about this new place in Manila called the Rockwell Center. Apparently, there were condominiums for sale there. I initially heard about the Rockwell Center from my priest-friend and life mentor, Monsignor Antonio 'Derps' Unson. You'll hear more about Derps later in the story. I was always interested in real estate, but I was very intrigued by how highly Derps talked about this particular real estate project. My interest peaked when he told me that the Lopez family owned the Rockwell Center. You see, it was a Filipino named Eugenio Lopez, Sr. who inspired an American named Robert Allen to become a multi-millionaire real estate investor. In case you haven't heard of Robert Allen, he is the best-selling author of many real estate and financial success books.

I had heard the incredible Lopez-Allen mentorship story two or three times before in my life. Mark Victor Hansen had talked about the story the night we met at the conference in 2003, and the Lopez-Allen story was also printed in one of the *Chicken Soup for the Soul* books. When I read that story for the first time, I got goose bumps! I found it so amazing that a Filipino actually mentored an American to become a millionaire. Not only was I amazed, but I also felt extremely proud. What a coincidence that I was Filipino — just like Mr. Lopez. It really got me seriously wondering whom I could inspire. It is important to note that Eugenio Lopez, Sr. died a long time ago, but many of the Lopez creations still exist. He left an incredible real estate legacy for his family, not to mention a conglomerate of

 Living a life of gratitude, abundance and purpose.

companies, which include the most powerful Filipino broadcasting company and the electric company that lights up the entire mega-metropolis of Metro Manila. With all the interesting things that I heard about the Lopez family, I decided that it was worth my time to check out the Lopez's newest addition to their enterprise, the Rockwell Center.

My family and I were staying at the Mandarin Hotel in Manila. After one night there, we were supposed to proceed to my home village of Pader, a few hours south of Manila. Anyway, instead of heading to Pader, we first decided to visit this intriguing Rockwell Center. My friend Derps arranged for us to see some of the rented units right away. He also did his best to get us hooked up with the Rockwell Center's professional sales team.

Now, you should really see the Rockwell Center — it is absolutely amazing! A beautifully developed, self-contained, mixed-use business, school and office community, the Rockwell Center has six very fancy, very tall, very exclusive residential towers. Among many outstanding facilities, there are sports and leisure clubs and a diverse shopping center. It has even become the new home to many business and government offices. All in all, the entire plaza is a luxurious, extremely high-end condominium community. I used to dream about going into places like this as a child, but I never thought that one day I'd actually be in the position to consider becoming an owner of a piece of such a property.

Anyway, there we were at the Rockwell Center, and we were seriously considering investing in one of their condominium units. How did this happen? True to form, Monsignor Derps reminded us to pray before we went ahead with any decision to purchase at the Rockwell Center. We did pray, and the answers became very clear. Before our family returned home to Canada, my husband and I put the required deposit for one of the Rockwell's *Manansala* units (Manansala is a famous Filipino architect). We thus became an official investor in one of the most prominent Lopez commercial properties. You may be wondering what this story has to do with the inspiration to write my book. Well, be patient, the juicy part is coming up.

After purchasing the Rockwell condominium and celebrating the 50th anniversary of my parents, our family returned to Canada and continued life as usual. My family knew I would be returning to the Philippines two months later for a very special mission. My parents' real 50th anniversary was in May. We celebrated it in March only because we wanted my daughters to be there while they were on school holidays. My parents didn't know it at that time, but I had planned to return to the Philippines on their actual anniversary. I found out that one of the perks that the Rockwell Center offers out-of-town investors is a certain number of free stays in one of their beautiful condominium units. I planned to surprise my parents with a few days stay in one of those units. I knew that they would be delighted.

 Living a life of gratitude, abundance and purpose.

Looking back, the whole scenario now appears so amazing to me. My parents spent most of their lives in a one-room, bamboo-floored *nipa* hut, as did I until the age of sixteen. We had no electricity and no real beds. We didn't even have a toilet or running water. We really lived in the poorest of circumstances.

I'm here to tell you that dreams do come true, my friends. I was able to astonish my parents with that Rockwell Center vacation — their daughter, who as a child used to sell fruits and vegetables and candies, had become an owner of one of the most expensive condominiums in the Philippines.

Surprising my parents and tying up the final details of the Rockwell investment were not the only reasons for that second trip to the Philippines that year. There was another reason I had returned home. The idea of writing the real *Tale of Juliet* was still bubbling in the back of my mind and I decided that I needed to explore it further. I thought the next step in the process was to find a little Filipino inspiration.

So, on that second trip to the Philippines, I set the intention to seek out a Filipino author. Strangely, I didn't even know any Filipino authors at that time and I had no idea how I would meet any. What I did know was that I had a clear and strong desire to figure it out. My intuition was pointing me in that direction and I had to follow it. Besides, I am a true believer in Divine Intervention and I knew that something would come across my path. Sure enough, something did. What follows next is really quite remarkable.

I decided to pay a visit to my priest-friend and mentor, Derps. This was after surprising my parents in Manila with the Rockwell condominium stay. Derps is always so generous and inspiring. The day we got together, he brought a bunch of books by his favorite authors to our meeting. He wanted to give me the books as a gift. Derps did not even know yet of my desire to meet a Filipino author and my intention to write a book. It was all very coincidental. One of the books he gave me that day was by a Filipino woman named Susan Romero-Vidal. It was self-published and entitled, *The Gospel According To My Kitchen Sink*. I didn't know it then, but this book and its author would become very special to me.

After my meeting with Derps, I took my armload of books and returned to where I was staying to get a good night's sleep. I guess the universe had other plans in store for me. Serious jetlag woke me up that night at around midnight. Wide-awake, I rolled over and decided to pick up the little 'Kitchen Sink' book. I am a speed-reader and most of the time I fast forward to the end of each book that I read. But this was not the case with this little book. As I peered at the words with bleary eyes, something compelled me to read it very slowly. I mean, I got the distinct sense that I should really immerse myself into this book. I felt so connected with the author. The way she wrote touched my heart and stirred powerful

 Living a life of gratitude, abundance and purpose.

emotions in me. I surprised myself by reading the entire book from cover to cover in one night. I fell asleep dreaming of my own book.

On the following day, I sent an urgent text message to Derps: "I need to talk to Susan Romero-Vidal. I feel we have a connection." Once again, Derps and Divine Intervention worked together to make our meeting possible. We were able to meet on the very next morning for breakfast. You can just imagine my excitement. What had begun as an intangible intention to meet a Filipino author was about to become a physical reality.

Let me tell you about Susan. She has a dynamite personality and an infectious enthusiasm. I must admit some people describe me in the same manner. Perhaps that is the reason we hit it off from the moment we laid eyes on each other. I felt like we were long lost friends reuniting — kindred spirits even. I told Susan about my secret dream to write a book and why I had sought her out. I even shared with her my fears about my English grammar. I was so happy and relieved when she admitted that she did not write perfect English either. Yet I tell you her book is well written because it was written from the heart. Susan shared the same advice as Mark Victor Hansen, "Write the book and let the editors do their job." She added, "Just don't let them touch your writing style."

You might not believe this, but Susan and I didn't part ways until around five o'clock in the afternoon of the following day. She slept over at the Rockwell condominium with me and we talked until two o'clock in the morning. We were just like teenagers. We even shared the earpieces of my CD player so we could listen to inspirational audio programs together. We shared and talked until very late that night. Early the following morning, we woke up and immediately put another inspirational CD on.

That one made all the difference. It was entitled *Millionaire Mind Secret Psychology of Wealth* by another of my mentors, a man named T. Harv Eker. It was his words that inspired us to take immediate action. I remember how Susan and I sat on the bed together and wrote the vision, mission and outline of the book that you are reading right now. At the Rockwell Center's Unit 9D Luna Condominium, twenty-four hours after meeting Filipino author Susan Romero-Vidal, the first draft of this book was born. The real *Tale of Juliet* was on its way to becoming a written reality.

Six months after that amazing experience with Susan, I invited her to come to Canada. In fact, I was able to sponsor her entire trip! The frequent flier points that I had accumulated over the years paid for her flight, and I took care of the rest of the details. Gifting a trip to Canada for this new friend and special angel in my life was beyond my wildest dreams as a once poor street vendor girl, and there I was actually making it happen.

 Living a life of gratitude, abundance and purpose.

Living a life of gratitude, abundance and purpose.

CHAPTER 2

HUMBLE BEGINNINGS

"Do what you can with what you have, with where you are."
THEODORE ROOSEVELT

The house I grew up in is probably very different from the ones you are familiar with. Actually, it wasn't a house at all. I lived in a hut made almost entirely of *nipa*. *Nipa* is an important plant where I come from. It is found in the forests of the Philippines and elsewhere in Asia. It can be used to build many things including the walls and roofs of dwellings. Some say that *nipa* is important because it provides a buffer against potentially ferocious storms and floods of that geographic region. You see, when it rains in the Philippines, it really pours! The storms are extremely frightening even though you're supposedly protected inside a dwelling.

I remember going to sleep on the bamboo floor of our one-room *nipa* hut during the typhoon season. The bamboo strands were only about one inch thick so you could clearly see through to the muddy ground below. I'd always be curled up tightly next to my brothers and sisters as we listened to the powerful gusts of wind howling loudly outside. There were never enough blankets for everyone. I think we had maybe two or three blankets to cover all of

 Living a life of gratitude, abundance and purpose.

us, and we only had a few pillows to share. Our blankets were old flour sacks sewn together. Sometimes in the middle of the night, my whole family would have to quickly bundle together in one area of the small room to avoid the leaks from our *nipa* roof.

We had no electricity in our home either. We relied entirely on the daylight or a little kerosene lamp at night. Our version of a kerosene lamp was simply an empty soda bottle full of kerosene (when we could afford it) with a home-made wick that dipped down into it. We were lucky if we had enough kerosene for an entire night. During the typhoon season, it was a huge challenge to do anything at night because without electricity it was absolutely dark. During the really bad night storms, I remember being able to see the wide eyes of my brothers and sisters as the lightning illuminated our surroundings. In the morning after a storm, we would sometimes wake up soaking wet. That usually meant the storm had completely torn off our roof! On the next day, my parents would have to find someone to help put the roof back on — or assist us in building a new one if it was too badly damaged!

We never knew what kind of devastation we'd find in the morning after a storm hit. Often, we would gingerly leave what was left of our hut and make a beeline for our main food source — the garden beside our home. It was especially sad whenever we found that our vegetables had been completely ripped apart by the typhoon. If we had no rice, we'd hungrily walk towards a local farm and pick bananas off the ground. The bananas that I picked were small and hard, almost like a potato. They needed to be boiled in order to be edible. There were usually quite a few bananas on the ground after a big storm. The wind knocked them down from the trees and the farm owners didn't really care because they had no use for these damaged bananas. We would take the opportunity and pick up as many as we could so they wouldn't be wasted and we could have extra food. Boiled bananas did not make the most delicious meals. Once we boiled the young bananas, we dipped them into salt, sugar or *bagoong* (fermented fish paste) for a meal in place of rice.

When any of us had to go to the bathroom, we'd first find a nice patch of ground well behind our hut. The spot I would choose had to fulfill one very special requirement — it had to be situated near soft leaves. Can you guess why? Yes, we didn't have any toilet paper. Now, in case you ever have to wipe yourself with a leaf, be sure that you don't choose the leaves of the sugarcane plant. Those leaves are horribly rough and can do a lot of damage down there if you use them. I'd instead recommend finding a spot with much softer leaves nearby. Can you believe I was aged sixteen before I lived in a place with a real flush toilet? What a luxury that was!

You're probably getting the picture of me living in extreme poverty. And this is how it really was. Our little (and I mean really tiny) rural village was not only poor but also quite remote. My parents barely finished a high school education. They fell in love at a very young age and started to have babies, babies and more babies! If you're thinking, "I wonder if they are Catholics," you're right. Now, we are not just Catholics; we are *fourteen* Catholics. Yes, you read it right, *fourteen* — twelve children and two parents. Wait until you meet my mother and father, they are just as petite as I am.

While most of us kids were pretty healthy, two of my siblings (one born before me and the other after me) passed away from unknown illnesses while they were infants. It was quite common for young children to die from unknown diseases when I was a child. With the horrendous poverty, there was a lack of medical attention available, so if an infant got very sick, the little one could eventually succumb to death. Each of us twelve children was delivered by what you might call a quack doctor. She wasn't even a qualified midwife. She simply relied on her knowledge of herbs and her skills at pushing on my mother's belly when the time was right. With twelve children, my parents kept themselves very busy!

We obviously had very little, but my mother and father still somehow got enough money together to put me in school. I was enrolled in the only kindergarten class in the nearest town to our home, the class usually only attended by the more affluent children. It was the kindergarten of St. Claire's Academy. My parents knew the value of a good education and they were determined to help me get one. Of course, we didn't have much money to speak of, but I was armed with a few reading sessions with my father.

Each day, I walked to school from our village. It was at least one hour away by foot. I wore a sky-blue and white school uniform with scuffed black shoes. I remember how muddy the unpaved road between our home and the school could get. It wasn't amusing. One of my sweetest recollections is how my father would carry me on his shoulders and take me to the nearest gravel road, from where we could hopefully get a form of horse-drawn transportation called a *kalesa*. This was my school bus.

I am proud to tell you that I finished kindergarten ranked third out of thirty students. It was my first taste of education and I loved the power of it. I also valued the experience of learning to be with the well-to-do children. I made lots of friends, but I must admit I envied most of them. I'm sure you can understand. They always had the money to get the things that I only dreamed of having. Despite my underlying resentment, I completed kindergarten successfully and had my first taste of how sweet education was. I was looking forward to more of it. At that young age, I felt so lucky and very thankful. Many other children of my age from our little rural village did not have the same privilege of early childhood education in a private school.

I became quite popular with some of the village folk. I often got invited to parties and social gatherings, and whenever that happened I showcased some of the skills that I learned from kindergarten. I recited prayers and poems, sang songs, read short stories, and I also

 Living a life of gratitude, abundance and purpose.

danced. I was not afraid of performing for the people. Often, they would entice me by giving me coins.

Whenever they played my favorite music, I would go to the middle of the stage, which was bare ground touching the earth, and would dance my life away. They'd start chanting, sometimes dictating what moves they wanted to see from me, and obediently I would follow their motions. The loud laughter echoing in my ears of the crowd enjoying themselves would make me perform even better. Meanwhile, a bunch of coins would be landing on the ground thrown by the excited onlookers. Eventually I'd stop dancing and pick them up. It always ended with full excitement for me because I would have collected more money for my little coin bank.

Unfortunately, my happy times at school would not last. Shortly after that wonderful kindergarten year, the situation in our family changed — more and more babies were arriving all the time. I watched in wonder as my siblings were born one after another. Sadly, my parents could no longer afford to send me to a private school. Nonetheless, there would be new adventures in store for me.

AN ENTREPRENEUR IS BORN — FILIPINO STYLE

The necessity to help my parents feed my younger brothers and sisters, combined with my sincere desire to someday reach higher education, led me in a new life direction. I was forced to become a

 Living a life of gratitude, abundance and purpose.

seven-year-old entrepreneur. At this young age, I did not know what the definition of the word 'entrepreneur' was, but I was convinced that it meant severe humiliation and major deprivation of playtime.

Picture yourself at seven-years-old. You see the kids your age playing games and having fun. You would love to join in the laughter, but you have to go to work. How would you feel? You see, while the little kids around me were fooling around, I was walking the neighborhood selling *pandesal* (small bread loaves), *talong* (eggplant), *bibingka* (rice cake baked using hot charcoal in a clay pot) and *Indian mango*. My circumstances changed — I no longer felt privileged. In my very young mind, my self-esteem went downhill fast.

You might have initially pictured me selling my wares around a North American styled neighborhood with one house very close to another. But this was not what my neighborhood looked like at all. Where I came from, the nearest neighbors would be hundreds of yards away. This is really true, my friends. I am not exaggerating. From where we lived in Pader, we could not see our nearest neighbors. Sometimes, the only landmark that there was another family out there at all was a banana grove or some mango trees — prime locations to build a *nipa* hut.

As I've mentioned, I was (and still am) very petite. This made carrying a massive *bilao* packed with goods on my head and a basket stuffed full of fruit slung from my shoulder pretty challenging. Did

I mention that I was very often barefoot? I would either have to walk for miles under the blazing sun or slosh through serious tropical rainstorms just to make a buck. It was very difficult, to say the least. Sometimes I worked with my mother and sometimes with my big brother Ohnie. I always hoped that there would be some farmers along my way that might need something from my heavy basket. In case there were people around, I'd chant or yell at the top of my lungs, "Ice *kendi!* (popsicles!) *pandesal!* (bread!) *isda!* (fish!)."

On the days when we sold *pandesal*, we had to get up especially early to pick them up. When I say early, I mean like four o'clock in the morning. As I said, our little village was way off the beaten track. The town of Lian, approximately one hour away by foot, was where the *pandesal* loaves were baked. My brother and I would pick up the *pandesal* in Lian and head directly back to our village chanting the whole way "*Pandesal! Pandesal!*" A good day was when we sold all our goods. This meant that we earned around twenty to thirty pesos — the equivalent of less than one dollar. Not much for several hours of walking around and yelling, but it was a lot to us at that time. Of course, our younger siblings would be very happy if there was some *pandesal* left over, so they could eat them. But if we had too many remaining, that meant we had lost the chance of earning some all-important profit so that we would have enough capital with which to buy goods the following day. By the time we finished our morning vending, it was almost always time to get ready to walk another hour to the elementary school.

 Living a life of gratitude, abundance and purpose.

Now, you might think that going to school at least meant our time as entrepreneurs was over for the day. Nope. Our day had just begun. My job was to bring a bag of *kendi* (candies) to school and spend the entire recess hour selling them piece by piece. At the end of the day, if I counted the change properly, I might earn an extra twenty-five cents and have one free candy for my snack. Keep in mind that I'd get a good scolding from my mother when I got home if all the candies were gone but I didn't have that extra twenty-five cents. She would either think my math skills were very poor or that I used up that money buying other snacks at school. Either way, she would not be pleased. And, oh my, I did not want to get caught lying to my mother. She instilled in all of us the value of honesty in a very unique way. I'll have to warn you, this next part is not very pleasant.

If any of my siblings and I ever got caught lying to my mother, it meant something awful. We'd have to lie on the ground or floor (whichever was handy), while she got a piece of a tree branch (freshly picked). She would whip us with that tree branch repeatedly until we confessed our dishonesty. On the days when she didn't have enough energy, she would pinch us on the upper torso or in the meatiest part of the leg. My mother was small but could be fiercely energetic. If we cried too loud after a beating, we would get some more, so we tried our best to suppress the tears. The hitting and pinching would often leave rainbow bruises. You know what I mean, those big red and yellow, blue and purple dark marks. Many times

 Living a life of gratitude, abundance and purpose.

this would lead to further embarrassment at school for me. If I wore my usual short school dress, the marks would be very evident. My classmates would look at me quite differently. Maybe they felt sorry for me, but my guess is that they had the impression I must have been a very bad person to receive such punishment. I know that my *Inay* meant well, but I can never really understand those beatings. By the way, *Inay* means mother in Tagalog.

There were a lot of pressures laid upon my mother to raise her children. We did not own any land to farm and there were no jobs available in the village that my father could take on to support his family. One of my father's cousins in Manila taught him how to drive and helped him find a job there as a bus driver. Manila was a good few hours away from our village. There were no telephones or other means of communication to keep my father and mother connected whenever he was in Manila. We never knew when he was going to show up with his earnings. He would only come home intermittently, perhaps two days in a month, not because he didn't care but because of the nature of his job. Meanwhile, my mother would be left wondering when she would next see my father. During such times, she was left to fend for all their children.

When we ran out of rice to eat, she would bravely approach our neighbors or relatives to borrow rice and would promise to pay them when my father returned. We would be lucky if they had some spare to lend us. Rice is the main staple in the Philippines. As

 Living a life of gratitude, abundance and purpose.

long as we had rice, we were okay. When we also had dried fish or meat, and vegetables to go along with the rice, we really considered that a bonus. Otherwise we would be happy with *bagoong* and sometimes when food was really scarce just a few grains of salt sprinkled on top of the rice. I can only imagine the constant worry of a mother with an out-of-town husband and left alone to take care of so many children when she did not have much to start with. She did her very best to make sure that we, her children, did not sleep with empty stomachs.

I grew up seeing my mother often doing some bartering. She always had something to sell. She also learned how to be a hairdresser 'village style' and would exchange her services for rice, chicken, eggs, fruits or vegetables. When I say village style, this was sort of a mobile salon. My mother would pack up all she needed as a hairdresser — scissors, curlers and other hairdressing necessities. She would travel to another rural village and park herself in one home with two or more ladies wanting their hair done. I remember tagging along with her, tired of walking but happy because whoever would host this haircutting session would usually feed us good food. I would also help her sort the curlers and other accessories. We washed the gadgets after each use, dried them, and ensured they were ready to use for the next session.

As I got older, the more responsibility was heaped upon my small shoulders. My vending territory expanded past our small neighborhood, which meant that I had to now cover a much larger area. My mother even discovered other ways of making money on the weekends. I was often sent with one of my younger siblings to Balayan, which was two towns away, to buy fresh fish in bulk. Again, we would leave home really early to get the first catch of the day fresh from the fishermen. Now, there was absolutely no chance to fool around on these morning trips. If we did, the fish would go bad and we'd be in serious trouble. On our way back from Balayan, we would pass by farms and buy vegetables to go along with the fish we were selling.

On the days when there were no fish available, our mother would send us to vend clothing materials. She often got the materials on consignment. Although I didn't appreciate it then, my mother was teaching me some very valuable marketing strategies. She told my younger brother Jose and me that the material was a 'big-ticket' item, unlike the fish, candies, fruits and vegetables that we usually sold. I have to note that at this time my big brother Ohnie started working on his own, harvesting sugarcane at the neighboring farms. So the next brother in line was Jose, who is four years my junior. I, the big sister, then became in charge of village selling.

Big-ticket items meant we no longer chanted and yelled out loudly. Instead, we were instructed that it was more appropriate to sell these items door-to-door. For that matter, my mother instinctively knew the best target marketing — she would tell us whose house to go to and when was the most opportune time. As I stated before, houses (or huts) in the rural areas of the Philippines are mostly made of *nipa* and have no doors on which to knock. Besides that fact, most of the time the occupants of the huts are outdoors tending their vegetable gardens or feeding their livestock (chickens, pigs or goats). So, this was a whole new kind of sales experience for me.

Now, I'm not sure what you're thinking, but it is important to note that I did not find this kind of direct sales any easier than the other selling method we were used to. It was even more embarrassing and time consuming than peddling along the village roadside. Firstly, I had to call on the occupants of the home. This was most uncomfortable when there were many neighbors lingering around the yard. Sometimes you would see mother-and-daughter pairs picking lice from each other's heads. With animals like cats and dogs moving about freely in rural areas such as ours, livestock surrounding the huts, and people sleeping on the floors with *banig* (woven mats), it was common for rural folks to have lice (or *kúto*, pronounced cutely as KUH-toh) on their heads. So picking lice is but part of the daily routine in the impoverished countryside of the Philippines.

Another thing common in developing countries like the Philippines is gathering together to chat or gossip. On such instances, for some reason, I could feel the gossip was about me. I do not know why I thought this way at that time, but perhaps it was because

 Living a life of gratitude, abundance and purpose.

I felt so embarrassed doing what I did. I would see children of my age playing and horsing around while my younger siblings and I were walking from village to village selling.

Sometimes I could overhear people saying, "Poor kids, they are so young," and then I would hear them say about my mother being mean to us for making us do what we were doing. At that young age, I knew that we did not have much of a choice except to obey our mother, but I would not be honest if I did not say there is a little resentment left in me. I had to get over my fear of being ridiculed by the villagers and instead focus on the skills of negotiating for better prices, which my mother taught me, so that I could sell. I learned a lot about door-to-door sales, and much of it would be of benefit in due time.

DIRECT DOG SALES

Have you heard of author Blair Singer's book entitled *Sales Dogs*? I had the privilege of meeting him in Vancouver. Well, he compares people's sales styles to different breeds of dogs. All I have to say is, "Mr. Singer, please take a moment to listen to my experience of sales dogs!" As far as I can recall, the incident happened on a partly cloudy day, sometime before noon. I think it was before noon or even earlier because my basket was still very full. Even though it was a little cloudy, I can still remember my skin feeling very hot in the sun. I was wearing flip-flops — beach slippers or thongs as you

 Living a life of gratitude, abundance and purpose.

might call them — and I wore a very tattered t-shirt and a pair of old plain shorts. In this outfit, certainly with the flip-flops, I tended to look like a boy, especially when I was very young.

Jose and I were engaged in our usual selling routine. We approached a house with the noble intention of selling some of our goods so our family could eat. The owner of this particular house on this particular day did not hear us approaching — but someone else did! As we were approaching the house and were ready to start yelling for the owner to know we were around to vend our goods, suddenly a ferocious looking dog came wheeling around the corner of the house, barking at the top of his lungs.

I was scared to death and instantly froze in my tracks. As the dog approached us, I quickly snapped out of it and began running as fast as I could in the other direction. Now, I did not know at the time that I was not supposed to run — a gesture that meant the beast had defeated you. I also didn't know that most dogs could surely outrun small children. I'm not sure either fact would have made a difference to me at that time anyway. I ran for my life, hanging on tightly to my basket full of goods. Spotting cover a few meters away, I leaped into a large patch of thorny bushes.

I had no idea where my brother ended up. I crouched down, shocked and trembling in the uncomfortable bushes. Thank goodness, the owner who had been tending his livestock a short

 Living a life of gratitude, abundance and purpose.

distance away heard the commotion. He came running to the rescue, calling off that crazy dog. Apologetically, he helped my brother and me gather our goods, which were now scattered haphazardly all over the ground. My heart was thumping and I was crying loudly. I thought this beast would eat me!

The owner told us that the dog was just mouthy but didn't really bite. This was of little comfort to me as I looked down at my legs now full of bloody scratches from the thorns. What a disaster! I could give up and go straight home to face my mother's scolding or I could gather up my courage and move forward with my day. Unfortunately, I was near the beginning of my vending shift and my basket was still very full of goods. The choice was clear. Instead of giving up and going home to my mother, I wiped my tears and continued vending. My job was to bring home money, not fear. I had two choices at that moment. I was unaware at the time, but this important (albeit traumatic) life experience would serve me well later in life. After we sorted out the situation, Jose and I made it a point to try to be still if ever we faced a ferocious-looking dog again. We also learned to arm ourselves with a large stick. This would serve as a barrier to any would-be attacker. We composed ourselves and moved on with our selling that day, scarred but a little bit braver.

 Living a life of gratitude, abundance and purpose.

CHAPTER 3

TEENAGE HUMILIATION

*"Decide what you want, and decide what you are willing
to exchange for it. Establish your priorities and go to work."*

H. L. HUNT

My mother was very smart — she always gave us choices. She used to say, "You can stay at home to help around the house or you can continue to sell *and* go to high school." When I was younger and I sometimes earned a lot more than I expected, I sort of developed a liking for selling. However, by the time I was a teenager, I was ready to be finished with the whole thing. Imagine yourself at a party where all of your friends are socializing and having fun. Instead of participating in the action, you are in a tiny booth in the corner of the celebration selling cigarettes, candies, gum, soda and other party snacks — well, this was my common situation as a teenager.

The parties that I am talking about are a way of life in most Filipino villages. Our town has a patron saint called John the Baptist. This saint is very popular. He is believed to grant wishes and cure sick people. Where I come from, it is tradition for people to request to have the patron saint's statue brought to their house. There is a

Living a life of gratitude, abundance and purpose.

long waiting list of up to five years or more if you want a particular date. Anyway, anyone who hosts this statue throws a party for a whole twenty-four hours. Sometimes all their life savings will be spent on feeding the people who attend the party.

Let me tell you, people come from all over the place for these functions. The hosts do this because of the goodness of the Lord, so they feel it is okay to spend all they have. In extreme cases, hosts even borrow money to fund these get-togethers. Everyone in the village is welcome to come, whether they are personally invited or not. That's the Filipino style of hospitality. We love to party and the festivities often last all night. No one goes to sleep. Instead, we stay up dancing and singing into the wee hours of the morning. A mobile amplifier is usually rented and music is played as loud as possible. Actually, the louder the music, the better the party. If the four villages surrounding the blast can hear the music, then it is at the perfect volume!

Young and old happily dance and sing at these parties. This meant a captive market for vendors like me. What could be better than a lot of people in one venue at the same time? Well, I knew what could have been better. I was a teenager and I desperately wanted to have fun, too. I wanted to join in the dancing and singing at those parties. I guess I could have left my booth for a little while, but I knew what would happen if I did that. My booth would have been mobbed for free stuff and I might as well have run away from home. God knows what punishment would have been in store for me then. I had no choice. If I wanted to further my education, there was no easy way out. I resigned myself to this embarrassing trade and tried to forget about my other options.

Matabungkay Beach

My mother was also very creative. In addition to selling at the local market and having a small booth at local celebrations, she heard some of the villagers were earning pretty good money selling fruits at a nearby resort called Matabungkay Beach. She told me that I would be coming with her to this beach. I was thinking, "Oh no, that's the beach where quite a few of my classmates live. Matabungkay Beach means more embarrassment."

On the first day when I was supposed to go and sell fruits with my mother in Matabungkay, I managed to come up with a good excuse to stay at home. I can't remember the excuse now, but it was good enough because she left me at home to care for my younger siblings. Don't get me wrong, the work at home could be just as hard as selling, but it was way less embarrassing. I had to do things like fetch water from the well (a twenty-minute walk from our house) and do the family laundry by hand.

For drinking water, we got it from an uncovered well a few feet deep by the same stream where we washed our clothes. We would use an empty oilcan as a bucket to fetch water. It would take many trips to fill up our reservoir barrel at home. I would roll a piece of cloth, about the same size as a regular bath towel, put it on top of my head, and over that place the three-quarter-filled can of water. As I was growing up (in age, not in height, that is), I did so many trips like this with a heavy load on top of my head, I wonder if it's possibly one of the reasons that I did not grow in height!

By the way, you might be interested to know that we washed our clothes by rubbing a bar of soap on the clothes, also by holding the clothes firmly and rubbing them between our wrists. We rubbed and rubbed until the dirt (or our skin) disappeared. We then used a *palo-palo* (small wooden paddle). We practically beat the garments to bits. We would then rinse them in the running water of the stream. Sometimes, I would get carried away playing in the water instead of washing clothes. It was so easy to while away the hours turning rocks over to expose the tiny rock crabs or teeny weenie shrimps that lived underneath.

If I weren't careful enough, however, it would be afternoon before I knew it and the clothes would be left unwashed. You and I both I know what would happen then — a good scolding from my mother. The threat of this consequence caused us siblings to become much smarter over time. We would hurriedly wash the clothes (the less rubbing and rinsing the better) so we could go swimming or have some fun catching those little stream creatures. That was how we played. We had to be smart and use efficient time management techniques so we wouldn't get caught.

It was great being able to stay at home, but I wasn't able to avoid the task of vending at Matabungkay Beach for long. I'll never forget one time when my mother came home from the beach, she was absolutely ecstatic. She brought home large pieces of roasted chicken, delicious smelling prawns and big chunks of barbecued pork. It was the leftover food from a foreigner's picnic that would have ended up being thrown away. Instead, he offered them to my mother and it fed our whole family. We were overjoyed and ate like we had won the lottery! And we even saved some leftovers for the following day's meal. *Bless your good heart, Mr. Foreigner. You made our family very happy that evening.* We never know how our little acts of kindness make a difference in someone's life. Keep this in mind if you ever travel to an underdeveloped country like the Philippines. Your acts of kindness will often have a ripple effect.

My mother made more money in Matabungkay Beach than in her usual sales areas. In part, this was because of the large number of foreign customers, but also because of a smart pricing strategy most Filipinos were trained to use. When the customer was a *puti* (white tourist), we Filipinos would double or even quadruple our asking price. Surprisingly, even when we quadrupled our prices, the tourists still thought the goods were good value and some even gave us extra money as a tip.

 Living a life of gratitude, abundance and purpose.

After my mother's amazing food fortune day, she really believed that selling in Matabungkay Beach would be our gold mine. Of course, I was still embarrassed to be seen by my classmates there, but I had no choice. If I wanted to continue my education, I had to go. That was all there was to it. So, I was on it. We only went to Matabungkay Beach in the summer and on weekends, thankfully. This meant I could spend all week planning a strategy on how not to be seen by my school peers.

The first time I went to Matabungkay Beach to sell fruits, I went with my aunt. Dragging a heap of goods behind us, we set off to this so-called 'gold mine' beach together. By lunchtime on this first day, I noticed that I was still carrying a very heavy load of mangoes while my aunt was on her second batch already. I tried to keep a good distance away from her and peddled on my own, but I guess I wasn't far away enough.

I figured that most customers thought we were together as a team. They probably assumed that I was her daughter so it didn't matter from whom they purchased the goods. Well, it mattered to me. What my aunt was selling was hers and what I was selling was for my family and me. I decided that if I wanted to pick up the pace I had to lighten my load. So I got rid of some of the cumbersome mangoes by depositing them in one of the stores. They were just too heavy to carry all at once. I watched my aunt and learned the art of approaching foreigners with broken English.

I decided to target those foreigners predominantly. I knew that I could get more money out of them. So, with a heavy load on top of my head and a basket full of fruits anchored by a sling on my shoulder, I bravely guided myself away from my aunt to the larger, more exclusive beach houses. I loved to watch those rich people relaxing on the big porches, reading magazines and sipping their favorite drinks.

Oh how I wished I could experience that someday. My mind would wander as I wondered how I could ever achieve a lifestyle like that. *Could I? Would I? Oops . . . I was dreaming again. I had better get back to work.* With the sea breeze blowing over my face, tiny feet digging in and out of the white sand, unmindful of the hot sun, off I went going back and forth in front of these large ocean-view houses chanting, "Mangoes! Sir! Madam!"

Oftentimes I would look up at the jet streams wondering where those planes were going. Little did I know that oneday my name would be *Jhet* and I too would be jetting all over this world of ours.

On some weekends, there were more mangoes available from the suppliers and we were able to double the amount we brought. To our disappointment though, most of the vendors like us had the same idea. This meant there was way more supply than demand. Remember economics class? We would sometimes return home with half a sack of mangoes and no food fortunes given to us by the tourists. Let me tell you, a bunch of leftover wasted mangoes made for a very

 Living a life of gratitude, abundance and purpose.

sad day. To avoid this problem, my aunt and I developed a new kind of strategy. We decided to introduce a product mix. Instead of selling only mangoes, we would offer different kinds of rice cakes, peanut brittle, bananas and any other in-season fruit. This was a bright idea. After implementing this strategy, our sales got better and better. Now, even if we didn't sell off all our goods, at least we would bring home a variety of leftovers to share with our families.

During these long arduous days of beach vending, I had to think up little challenges to stay interested. One of my motivations was to sell out the goods as fast as I could so that I could play on the beach. My lucky weekends were when I was able to sell out all my goodies by around three o'clock in the afternoon. Then I would have some time left to soak myself in the ocean. It would be an even greater bonus if I did not see any of my schoolmates. Unfortunately, a sold-out situation didn't happen very often. Most of the time, I barely had any chance to play. Even so, I always made a point of dipping my tired feet in the salty ocean water.

By the time we finished our vending day, the last-trip transportation to our neighborhood was about ready to leave. On my way home, I always wondered what my classmates were doing. I bet they were playing or keeping busy doing their homework, I thought. Good for them. How I wish I could do such things during the weekends. While they were having fun and relaxing, I was helping my family make ends meet. I was also paying for my own schooling

 Living a life of gratitude, abundance and purpose.

and, though I didn't appreciate it at the time, I was getting an even more valuable education simultaneously.

BAGOONG DAYS

The money I made vending at Matabungkay Beach allowed me to resume attending St. Claire's Academy. This was the school where I first started kindergarten many years earlier. Not only was this the one private high school in our area, but it was also a Catholic school. My parents were happy about that because they truly believed in combining a good education with a sound spiritual foundation. At St. Claire's, I was reunited with some of the well-to-do classmates whom I met during kindergarten. My big brother Ohnie, who was four years my senior, also attended the same school.

I am not exactly sure just how rich my St. Claire's classmates were, but I knew that Ohnie and I were the poorest of them all. I also knew that none of the other students were doing what we had to do just to get an education. Not only did we live the farthest from school, but we were probably the only two children at St. Claire's Academy who had to walk several miles (rain or shine) to get to class. We were also certainly the only kids whose before-school assignment was to sell fruits and vegetables from their home garden.

Sometimes I would bring boiled bananas, corn or peanuts to school to sell. Although this was against my will, my mother thought that selling to my well-to-do classmates would be easy. On one hand, it was good because most of our merchandise would be sold by lunchtime. On the other hand, I felt that they looked down on me as their poor classmate. Sometimes I sensed that I really didn't belong in this private school. My parents and I had to work extra hard to save up to pay for private schooling even while there was a public school in the area. But I could not disobey my mother's wishes.

During our early morning selling shifts, before school started, Ohnie and I would usually take our goods to the market or to one particular corner store in town. We would leave them there on consignment. We would feel very lucky if they were sold by the end of the school day. My mother used to give us a list of what to buy with the proceeds from our daily sales. When everything on consignment was sold, it meant that we could buy all the items on her list. We bought things like eggs, dried fish, *bagoong*, salt, sardines, kerosene and rice. This would help feed our ever-growing family. If we were really lucky, we might even have an extra few cents allowance for the following day.

I'd like to note that these fruits and vegetables that we were selling were by no means excess. Our growing family could actually have consumed them all for our own everyday needs, but the truth was that we needed other important basic foodstuff. For instance, we needed dried fish and eggs for our school lunch. Having vegetables with lunch was our last resort. At this time, my regular school lunches

 Living a life of gratitude, abundance and purpose.

consisted of a good portion of rice wrapped in a banana leaf and topped with a tiny piece of dried fish.

Sometimes instead of the fish I would get a quarter piece of very flat egg. The egg would be scrambled and fried as flat as a Dutch pancake or a French crêpe. Sometimes there would be neither fish nor egg but instead a tiny drop of the pungent *bagoong*. On *bagoong* days, I would purposely eat apart from the rest of my classmates. I knew that if the other students saw how little I had for lunch and exactly what I ate, they would talk about me and I would be even more humiliated.

THE CHEESES OF ST. CLAIRE

I endured many challenges and humiliations as a poor student attending school in the Philippines. Some of the things I faced may be quite different from what you might have experienced during your school days. However, even though things were extremely difficult at times for me, I do have some fond memories of my time in school.

I remember one moment in particular. I usually didn't have any food allowance for snack time at school. When recess came, my classmates would run excitedly to the school canteen to get their favorite treats, while I would have to settle for a boiled banana, a piece of corn or a fresh cucumber from our garden. You've heard the saying cool as a cucumber, right? Well, this tiny uncut cucumber was far from cool. Nowadays, with the rise of health consciousness it would be cool, but certainly not then.

There was this one classmate of mine, though, who must have noticed my longing glances once in a while. Her name was Cecile and she came from a well-known family in town. If I remember right, her aunt and uncle owned St. Claire's Academy. Cecile would often buy these cheese curls for snacks. You know the kind — the yummy, puffy, cheesy, crunchy snacks.

Cecile was often kind enough to share a few with me. Man, those cheese curls tasted good! I loved cheese, or anything with cheese on it for that matter, but we never got any cheese at home. Oh how I wished I could buy a whole pack of cheese curls all for myself. Of course, I didn't have enough money to do that. Therefore I tried my hardest to be well liked by Cecile, so that I could have a taste of her delicious cheese curls.

Once in a blue moon, there would be food brought to school. I'm not exactly sure why it was there, but perhaps it was foreign aid sent to the Philippines after an earthquake or typhoon. Among the food items, there were these special cans I would get to bring home to my family. They were about four times the size of a tuna can and were filled with something delicious — cheese! They were from Holland, I think, and I could never get enough of this stuff. Oh how

I loved those cheese cans. I wished I could eat the whole thing myself, but of course I had many brothers and sisters to share with. It was perhaps that Holland cheese that led to me falling in love with and marrying a Dutch man later in my life.

Years later, when I first moved to Canada with that same Dutch man as my husband, I would buy a few packages of those cheese curls every time I shopped. I ate them whenever I could. I still crave for them once in a while and this craving always leads me back to the memories of my food-deprived childhood and that nice girl who shared her cheese curls with me.

Now when I munch cheese, most especially during family picnics or on long drives, I tell my husband and children why I love cheese so much. They understand my food-deprived past. *It has been a while, but the memories are still vivid at times. Every time I think about my past, I am full of gratitude for my present lifestyle — what a change in my life! It is now a major part of my life's purpose to do something to make a difference in the lives of all food-starved and education-deprived children.*

One of my most precious childhood memories is that of our school retreats. Once every few months, our class would spend an entire day inside the church next door to our school. We would all walk over to the church with a nun or a priest presiding over us. It was during these times when I felt that I could pour out all my

 Living a life of gratitude, abundance and purpose.

dreams, longings, aspirations and heartaches to God. I sincerely looked forward to those special intimate moments with my creator. There was something peaceful about handing over my worries to God, who's bigger than all my worries. I highly recommend it to everyone.

I continued vending in Matabungkay Beach until I graduated from high school at the age of sixteen. As far as I know, I successfully managed to keep my embarrassing trade a secret from my peers. My fear of being exposed was very real then, but I simply made my dream of education more real than my fear of being seen by my friends. I guess I understand now that the lessons I learned at this young age have certainly helped me tremendously to achieve far greater things in life. I'd have to say that as embarrassing as those fruit and vegetable selling experiences were, they fuelled a fierce entrepreneurial spirit in me. This spirit has been the root of my business success. *Thank you, Inay, for teaching me the gift of entrepreneurship.*

Even though I was extremely busy working a challenging selling job while attending high school, I still graduated as one of the top ten students in my class. If I could boast a little more here, I'd tell you that I even received a special honorable mention for garnering the highest grade in the national college entrance examination in our district. This high-grade achievement energized my already strong desire to pursue a college education. However, with our financial situation the way it was, I didn't know then just how I could ever make that dream a reality.

 Living a life of gratitude, abundance and purpose.

CHAPTER 4

DOORS OF OPPORTUNITY

"Nothing can take the place of persistence. Persistence and determination alone are overwhelmingly powerful."
CALVIN COOLIDGE

My father became the family driver of a very well-known and moderately wealthy family in our province. This family had ten children and was almost as big as ours. Once in a while, one of the sons (who also happened to be a well-respected priest) would ask my father to drive him to and from his appointments. This man's name was Monsignor 'Derps' Unson.

Derps was a slim, smart looking man. It could have been his glasses that made him look smart, or it could have been the fact that he really was smart. Derps was an incredible scholar. He graduated from college at the top of his class. His favorite subject was philosophy, which he mastered at the young age of nineteen. He was sent by Archbishop Rufino Cardinal Santos to Rome to do a post-graduate course in Canon Law. All in all, it was clear to me that this man was really quite remarkable. He was tall for a Filipino and he towered over me. Now, you must understand, Derps is one serious looking guy. When he looks at you, it feels like he is dissecting your soul.

Living a life of gratitude, abundance and purpose.

Obviously this can make him quite intimidating — at least that's what I thought.

In light of Derps' uniqueness, I am so amazed by what my father did. Are you curious? I already mentioned that my father would drive Derps to and from his appointments, right? Well, one day, on one of their trips together, my father did a very spirited act. His bravery on that day changed my life forever. My father got the courage to share one of his most troubling concerns with the solemn priest. "I have a daughter who just graduated from high school," he said, "and I already have my eldest son enrolled in an engineering school. I don't think I can afford to send my daughter to college." He took a deep breath before continuing, "She is smart and she really has a big dream. Do you think you can help?" That moment must have touched the heart of Derps and with a curt nod he put some plans into motion that would alter the course of my life.

I can still vividly remember meeting Derps for the first time. I was an undersized, self-doubting sixteen-year-old girl at that time. Derps brought us into this expensive looking restaurant and generously asked us to order whatever we wanted from the menu. "Hmmm," I thought, "it must be nice to have a lot of money." As far as I know, I appeared to be a dark-skinned (too much exposure to the sun along Matabungkay Beach), malnourished-looking girl from the province. But I guess Derps must have seen something else in me that day when we first met. He asked me lots of questions and I answered them to the best of my ability. I really can't recall exactly what he asked me now — I think I was pretty nervous. What I can remember is that he told me, "You are smart and you have tremendous potential. I have a friend at La Concordia College and we'll see if you can apply for a scholarship there." I was stunned — La Concordia is an exclusive Catholic school for girls. Exclusive *and* expensive!

I was amazed at his positive comments about me and my self-esteem soared skywards. Derps didn't even know me, yet he believed in my potential. His compliments made me feel very special indeed. Derps was a very powerful and extremely impressive figure. I walked into that meeting with Monsignor Derps Unson an apprehensive, anxious young girl, and I walked out inspired to be more than what I thought I could ever be. Derps had that inspiring effect on me. What an angel. *That moment in my life with Derps is one of the reasons you are reading this book. I want to share my inspiring message of hope with as many people as will be open to what I have to offer. I yearn to make a positive impact in many people's lives, just like what Derps did for me back then.*

I was even more impressed when my father brought me to their posh residence in the city to meet the rest of the priest's family. They lived in this beautiful gated house with separate servant quarters and a few luxurious-looking vehicles in the driveway. I got to see up close how their family lived. Before this visit, I especially remember

  Living a life of gratitude, abundance and purpose.

noticing how the whole Unson family would go to church on Sundays together. I'm not sure exactly why I noticed this particular fact. Perhaps I made a note to myself that rich people could be spiritual too, or perhaps I was simply impressed by this family who appeared very devout. I later learned that the Unson's helped many underprivileged people, churches and charitable institutions. In fact, just recently, my father told me how this family extended their help to our family in yet another touching way.

My father first applied for the job with Mamay Peping, the father of Derps. *Mamay* in my province means Grandfather. Some people simply called him Mamay, which is a great sign of respect. On the day Mamay first told my father that he had the job as their family driver, my father decided to take a big risk. It may not have been the greatest idea on his first day, but he decided to ask a big favor from his new employer anyway. He carefully told them that my brother (who was enrolled in an engineering course at that time) might need some financial help every now and then.

Continuing on, my father said he sometimes worried when my brother's tuition fee was due or when extra engineering supplies were needed and there was no money coming in. He wanted to know, if money was needed to help my brother out but it was not payday yet, was it possible to get an advance? The question was pretty courageous for a new employee, don't you think? My father's employer immediately replied, "I understand your situation. If you ever need something, just let me know, no matter what time of day or night." This is pretty incredible, but it isn't even the best part.

As fate would have it, my brother showed up late one night needing an engineering tool right away — a slide ruler. My father's monthly salary as a driver was barely enough for the rest of us, and his money was normally gone before the next payday. My father knew his employer had gone to bed hours earlier but decided to put his previous words to the test. He knocked on Mamay's door and expressed the need of my brother. The employer was quick to cooperate. He kindly gave my father the money and between them they agreed it would be deducted from my father's next paycheck. Are you ready for the astonishing part?

The next payday came and my father noticed that he had received a full paycheck. He immediately called this to the attention of his employer. He reminded Mamay to take out the advance money that was borrowed for my brother's earlier needs. With a smile, Mamay said this was my father's bonus pay and to not worry about it. He also announced that my father would be receiving a free sack of rice monthly. What a gift! From then on, we never have had to worry again about borrowing rice from one of our neighbors or relatives. Bless their good hearts. A sack of rice regularly every month is what our family needed to survive. That meant that our family would have extra money for the growing expenses of school supplies and other basic necessities.

 Living a life of gratitude, abundance and purpose.

LA CONCORDIA COLLEGE

My angel, Derps, the son of my father's employer, graciously arranged for me to take the La Concordia College entrance examination soon after our first meeting. If I did well at this exam, I would be on my way to attending this prestigious Catholic school for girls, on scholarship. Oh, how I studied so hard! I was not very confident at that time. The standard of education from the province is always a lot lower than in the city. This school has a higher standard for sure, I thought. I also prayed ardently: *Dear God, please help me. Please intercede for me. I need this education. My parents are so very poor. This exam is my ticket to a college education. I promise to help my brothers and sisters if you please help me pass this test.*

Early during the morning of the entrance examination, I visited the school chapel and prayed fervently. Prayer always seemed to calm me down. Well, the exam came and went with no real hiccups, but I still had a few days to wait before I got my results. Those few days felt like an eternity. Day and night I talked to God, remembering the proverb, *ask and you shall receive.*

To my amazement, I passed with flying colors! This good fortune began another amazing chapter of my life — a chapter similar in some ways to my past and very different in other ways. Incredibly, I was one of the few poor students to whom La Concordia granted a scholarship. Derps and this exclusive school (run and managed by

 Living a life of gratitude, abundance and purpose.

the Daughters of Charity) opened a big door of opportunity for me and I was filled with gratitude. Not only did I receive a scholarship to study at La Concordia, but I was also granted *intern working student* status. As you know, my parents could not afford to pay for my boarding house, so in order to afford to live there I had to work while I studied. Challenging, yes, but I vowed to myself that since this was one of the biggest breaks that I had ever gotten so far, I would do whatever it took to maintain the scholarship. A completely free college education. Wow, I could not have asked for more.

I found out that life wouldn't be totally easy at La Concordia. In order to stay on as an intern working student, I had to maintain a certain academic grade level and I had to work for my food and lodging. This meant that I was assigned several tasks on a daily basis. At first, I found it difficult to wake up as early as five o'clock in the morning to get my before-school work done, but I soon got used to it. There were many different chores to do and each of the intern working students would take turns doing them. Sometimes I would work in the laundry room, manually scrubbing linens for an hour or two. At other times, I would help in the kitchen preparing food, or be assigned to wash, clean or scrub. It seemed like there was never any shortage of manual labor assigned to us. There is a lot involved in running a well-managed school, I learned.

Our dormitory at La Concordia was one great big room, massive actually, with many single beds. There were no dividers between

 Living a life of gratitude, abundance and purpose.

the beds, meaning we could pretty much see what everyone else was doing at any given time. This didn't bother me that much since I had no privacy in my old one-room family hut either. I can't remember how many shower stalls and toilets there were, but I do remember that we had to wake up early and get into the queue, otherwise face a long wait. There were approximately thirty of us. Within this great big room was a great big table, surrounded by chairs. The table was for the students to use for studying.

There was a strict curfew in the dormitory. Every evening by ten o'clock the lights had to be off. If we wanted to study past the curfew hours, we had to use our flashlights. This was not normally allowed, but we could get away with it sometimes, especially if we took good care to cover ourselves well with blankets and turn the flashlight on only after the covers were neatly covering us. One wouldn't want to disturb the other sleeping students.

Above us on the second floor were the nuns' quarters. There were stairs connecting our dorm to the second floor, but these were accessible only to the nuns. The nuns often made rounds to make sure everyone was studying during the study time and not distracting other students. There was never any loud talking or music allowed, period. There was also a separate TV room in the dormitory. Movies were shown once or twice a month as a treat. There was a bell in the morning, usually around five o'clock, for the group of intern working students who had to go to their assigned areas for work that early.

 Living a life of gratitude, abundance and purpose.

Once again, I observed that I was the poorest among the working and non-working students. I often heard the other interns complain about our accommodations and bellyache about the food at La Concordia. I couldn't believe it! Compared to what I was used to (a one-room hut without a bed of my own), this was a big step up. I was very grateful for everything I saw around me. What a great privilege. There was a flush toilet, not to mention three nutritious meals a day, and snacks in between those meals. What else could I want? There were no soda-bottle kerosene lamps either. The college had constant electricity. And the best part was that the college chapel was adjacent to our dormitory.

Holy Mass was said early in the morning, every day. On the days when we were not assigned a task, we were obliged to attend Holy Mass. I didn't mind at all. I always found it so peaceful, and attending the services gave me time to meditate and talk to God. In addition to the Holy Mass, we also attended other regularly scheduled retreats facilitated inside the chapel. Sometimes, we would visit the Daughters of Charity Provincial House located in the outskirts of Manila.

This was an extra special treat for me. There was a beautiful garden at the Provincial House where we could sit all day and meditate or pray. I found such peace and tranquility in the solitude and power of my silent prayers. I further developed my already strong faith in God and in spiritual renewal. Throughout my prayers, I never forgot to

 Living a life of gratitude, abundance and purpose.

thank God for all his gifts to my family and me. All in all, things started out pretty well for me at La Concordia, but they were soon to get even better.

Sister Eliza

Initially, I really wanted to be a nurse, but at that time La Concordia College did not offer a scholarship for nursing students. One of my choices was a four-year commercial business science course. This was an okay choice, but I wanted to finish school as soon as I could so that I could find a job and help my parents financially. Four years seemed like an awfully long time to be in college. Besides, my parents still had to pay for the education and other basic necessities of my growing brothers and sisters, which meant they needed help fast. With this in mind, I chose a two-year medical secretarial course instead.

I started to notice something around this time in my life — my prayers were almost constantly being answered now. Each time I'd ask for something, it would inevitably show up in one form or another. Let me tell you more about what I mean. Aside from our rotation tasks, each of us 'working students' was assigned a particular department to take good care of. That meant we did all the jobs needing to be done so that our own special department could operate efficiently. This included keeping the department clean and tidy. Do you remember that I wanted to be a nurse? Well, I was officially

 Living a life of gratitude, abundance and purpose.

assigned to the school medical clinic. Imagine! It wasn't nursing, but it was the closest thing to nursing at La Concordia. Something else made this medical clinic assignment particularly special. It was here that I met the next incredible angel of my life.

Her name was Sister Eliza Cervantes. She was a young, intelligent nurse who also happened to be a student nun. Like so many other people who have touched my life, Sister Eliza has a very good heart. She happened to be in charge of the school medical clinic. This enabled us to get to know one another really well. Sister Eliza was about ten years older than me. Like Derps, she wore glasses and she also had a very intelligent look.

What I remember most about her was the good-natured, compassionate look in her eyes, and that she was full of wit and wisdom. She had a great sense of humor and seemed so down-to-earth — especially when compared to the older, stricter nuns that ran the school at that time. She was open-minded, very understanding and had good listening ears. She was polite, kind and generous.

I really can't say enough good things about Sister Eliza. I truly believe her true calling was to be of service to God and to help other people. She was from a well-to-do family and probably could have done anything she liked. Instead, she decided to enter a special sisterhood called the Daughters of Charity.

 Living a life of gratitude, abundance and purpose.

Sister Eliza and I became very close working together in the La Concordia medical clinic. I always felt I could be my true self with her. Being so far away from home often made me lonely, and Sister Eliza really listened to me during those difficult times. She offered me support and once in a while wrote encouraging notes and poems to me. I guess I thought of her as a mother-figure as well as a friend. I can honestly say that Sister Eliza was a true inspiration. She loved to play the guitar and would often strum a tune when I was around doing my chores at the clinic. Her music seemed to sooth my soul. Like Derps, Sister Eliza's presence made me feel very special.

Now, Sister Eliza did more than befriend me, she named me! As you might remember, my real name is *Julieta*, or *Juliet* for short, but now everyone calls me *Jhet* — thanks to her. And the name suits me perfectly. Sister Eliza often wrote little notes to me with words of inspiration. Well, one day I got a note that was a little different from the rest. This particular note read, "Juliet, you are small but you move very fast. Let me call you Jet as in jet plane!" At first I wasn't so sure about being named after a plane, but Sister Eliza's note went on to say, "Don't worry. To make it less obvious, we'll put an 'h' in between J and e. This will make you Jhet." Thus my name was born! I adopted it immediately, and with enthusiasm I was writing it everywhere. Years later, even my parents started calling me Jhet instead of Juliet. When you meet me, you can tell that this name perfectly suits me. In fact, it has manifested itself throughout my life's journey. I'll tell you more about that later.

 Living a life of gratitude, abundance and purpose.

Two years after starting at La Concordia and meeting Sister Eliza, I graduated as a medical secretary — not the business-degree graduate that I originally *wanted to be*, but what I believed I *needed to be* in order to more speedily help my financially-constrained family. Remember Derps? Well, throughout my years at La Concordia, whenever his schedule permitted, he would visit just to check up on me. I kept him posted on the major events in my life. I always sought his wisdom and advice, and I always felt special in his presence. Derps would often let me know his thoughts on any decision that I had to make, and more often than not, his intuition would prove correct. How blessed I was to have both Derps and Sister Eliza — two angels for one young girl.

After La Concordia College, I continued on my life's journey and years later ended up in Canada, where I currently live. Unfortunately, Sister Eliza and I lost touch over the years. But because she was one of the people who inspired me and impacted my life in such a great way, I wanted to track her down. I really yearned to tell her how much she meant to me. I wanted to say: *Thank you Sister Eliza for the gift of your friendship and for giving me my name Jhet. You were perfectly right. Jhet suits me very well and has become a self-fulfilling prophecy as I have jetted around from place to place in my life. I love you.*

In the summer of 2004, out of the blue, a friend from the past named Annabel called me. She is Sister Eliza's niece. The last time

 Living a life of gratitude, abundance and purpose.

Annabel and I saw each other was approximately eighteen years ago in the Philippines, so I was shocked by the call. She broke some incredible news to me — Sister Eliza was in Canada! Unbelievably, I found out that Sister Eliza was at her brother's home and he lived just a thirty-minute drive away from where we live. I decided then and there I had to reunite with this long lost friend. How amazing that she should resurface in my life after all these years. It is important to note that I was seriously considering writing this book at that time and her re-emergence in my life seemed to be a sign that I should go ahead with my plans. I've learned to pay attention to the signs of the Divine.

I'll always remember our reunion well. I was so excited to see her and the meeting was wonderful. We were able to reconnect and get caught up on all the happenings in each other's lives. She told me that she had been assigned to a very poor village in one of the islands in the Philippines on the Pacific side. In fact, it is the same island province where my father was originally from — Catanduanes in the Bicol region. Over the years, she had also been assigned to larger, more modern communities and colleges. More recently, Sister Eliza opted out of these assignments and requested to go back to the poor missionary work she used to do. She believes that being around the very poor is where her true calling is. I commented that she would probably have a hard time adjusting to live in the Philippines after her trip to Canada, where she experienced the comfort, good food and relaxing North American lifestyle. She told

 Living a life of gratitude, abundance and purpose.

me that she would not have a hard time adjusting at all because it brings her such great joy to be of help to the poorest people. Amazing, isn't it? She truly has dedicated her life to serving others.

I even got to show Sister Eliza my home — Sister Eliza was so proud of me. You have to remember that when we met each other during my college days, I was the poorest student of La Concordia, and here I was years later with a beautiful house and a wonderful family. She was so very happy to see me again and to see that I had been blessed with so much. I felt very privileged to meet Sister Eliza's brothers and their wives, as well as her nephews and nieces after all these years. She has an extraordinarily kind-hearted family. It was an amazing reunion with Annabel and Sister Eliza and their families. Of course, the highlight was seeing Sister Eliza — the creator of my name Jhet. What a delightful friendship I found in her and how thankful I am that she graced my life with her presence.

Dr. Bill — The Great Man

Soon after I graduated, there were a few of us medical secretaries from La Concordia who had our clinical practicum in an upscale hospital situated in an affluent area called Greenhills, right in the heart of Metro Manila. This hospital was the well-respected Cardinal Santos Memorial Hospital. Every day, before proceeding to my assigned duties, I would go to the chapel and pray that I could get a job after I finished the clinical practice. I figured that ardent prayer

 Living a life of gratitude, abundance and purpose.

and strong intention really helped bring good things to me in the past, so why change my methods now?

I always tried to do my very best, no matter what tasks were assigned to me. My supervisors noticed my diligence and this fact contributed to an answer to my prayers. After six weeks of practice, I was hired. In fact, I was asked to start with the job right away. It was here that I really bloomed. I learned and grew as a person. Oh, and did I mention that I also fell deeply in love? During my eight years of employment in that Greenhills hospital, I met many wonderful friends and inspiring mentors whom I will never forget. That period of growth shaped my character and helped me through the challenges of adult life.

I first worked as an admitting secretary at the hospital and a few months later was promoted to the post of telephone operator. I climbed the ranks quickly. After a short time as an operator, I got promoted to the post of cardiovascular technician. That isn't where my good fortune stopped and I soon received yet another promotion. This would be the big one. I was proudly advanced to become the executive secretary of the medical director. My promotions all seemed to happen at the speed of lightning. I was propelled upward just like a jet plane!

I am very fortunate to have known and worked for the medical director at that time, Dr. Juanito B. Billote. He was highly

 Living a life of gratitude, abundance and purpose.

intellectual, very generous and a man of good humor. I can honestly say that he is one of the persons whom I most admire. A graduate of the University of the Philippines and the famous Harvard Medical University, Dr. Bill (as many fondly called him) is well-known in the Philippine medical community. He has a very dynamic personality. Aside from being the medical director at the Cardinal Santos Memorial Hospital, he held different key titles, was affiliated with many medical associations and had an extremely busy schedule.

Keeping up with his high standards kept me very active. In spite of Dr. Bill's hectic schedule, he always had time to crack a joke or share some of his experiences with me. He also felt comfortable enough to share his hopes and dreams, his love for music and his sincere interest in poems. He even told me stories about his pets. One of the best lessons he taught me was the power of delegation and generosity. This lesson was very helpful to me later in life when I started a business of my own with employees working for me.

As secretary to the medical director, I became a sort of VIP. All of the doctors wanting to have their internship and residency programs, private practices or affiliations with the hospital, had to go through our office. They would submit their applications and would then sometimes sit and chat with me while waiting for their interviews. In addition to all the work that I did for Dr. Bill, I also coordinated weekly presentations for the hospital's medical staff. As part of the medical staff's continuing education, different pharmaceutical companies would send their sales representatives to host video presentations at the hospital. These reps would show the staff new products and different medicines and vaccines. I did much of the scheduling and organization for these presentations.

It was neat because I got to know most of the physicians and their secretaries before they even got on board at the hospital. I was very proud of my position and my boss Dr. Bill. I loved my job and I stayed with it for seven full years. Working in the field of medicine allowed me to interact with many different kinds of people. These people had high levels of intelligence, education and more affluence than anyone I'd ever seen before. I fitted in easily with them and started to believe that it really didn't matter where I came from, I could be part of that kind of group. Once I interacted with and made many friends in the medical profession, I felt different. My bar had been raised and I continued to increase my self-confidence.

WEARING TWO HATS

My job as Dr. Bill's secretary was very stable. Even though I really loved working for him, I yearned for more education. After much thought, I decided that I would enroll in night school to pursue a business degree. However, when I saw the night class schedule, I developed some serious fears and was not sure if I should go for it. The schedule showed that I would have to leave the hospital office two hours earlier than the usual time. I feared that if I

 Living a life of gratitude, abundance and purpose.

approached the hospital administration about my plans, they might not approve my request and I might even lose my job. And what about Dr. Bill, what would he think? However, I remained focused on the big picture of what I was trying to attain. I wanted to be more than a secretary. I felt I needed to have a four-year business course in my résumé. I decided that I'd better let him know first. I knew that he had a good heart and would tell me what he thought was best. I felt afraid to talk with him, though. I didn't know what I would do if he rejected my plan. But I went for it anyway.

One morning, when Dr. Bill was inside his office, I finally found the courage to tell him about my interest in pursuing a four-year college education. I told him that I wanted to be more than a medical secretary. To my surprise, Dr. Bill easily understood and fully supported me. He encouraged me to go after my dream to finish a four-year commercial science course. This next part of the story shows Dr. Bill's big heart. Out of his pocket, he offered me extra money to pay for my schooling.

I graciously accepted and this extra pay helped me pursue my business course while continuing to share my earnings with the rest of my family. I felt like I had received another scholarship — working fewer hours *and* receiving higher pay! I would sometimes feel guilty accepting the money, but I knew that it was necessary at that time. Dr. Bill's generosity made it possible for me to pursue my dream of higher education. I am sure that every person who used to work for

 Living a life of gratitude, abundance and purpose.

him will share a similar story of his kindness and extraordinary unselfishness. He is another of my angels. He and his beautiful wife Lilet, who is also a physician, don't have any children of their own but they have helped and touched so many lives. *Dr. Bill, I will be forever grateful to you for your kindness and generosity.*

Wearing two hats was quite challenging at times. I was an executive secretary during the day and a full-time business student at night. I do not know how I managed. I believe the main thing that kept me focused was my long-term vision and my big dream of a higher education. Another big credit goes to Chris, my beloved boyfriend at the time. He played an important role in helping me realize my dreams. Chris gave me hope and love when I needed it most and was a continual source of inspiration.

I needed moral support to help me get through those demanding times, and he was really there for me. I was so much in love with him and felt so inspired by that love. He would pick me up from school just about every day. He even helped me out when necessary with my homework, most especially with English and essays. He was dedicated and he supported me at all times. You'll hear more about Chris in the next chapter. Our love story is one of my favorite subjects. But first, I'll tell you more about wearing two hats.

My professors were very cooperative and really understood my situation as a working student. Whenever there was a conflict with my schedule, like if an examination date fell on the same day as an executive meeting at the hospital where I was needed to take the minutes of the meeting, I would ask my professors for flexibility. They were very understanding and cooperative, and I would often get special arrangements made for me.

For example, they would have separate exam sittings for me and offer extensions if needed. I would explain to them that I was unable to take the test at a particular time because of my work schedule and would ask if they'd be willing to give it to me at a later date, and sometimes I'd simply ask for an extension for a big project. They always accommodated my reasonable requests. Asking for what you want is a great way to get it, I learned. Things were going really well in my life. I had a great job, was pursuing my education and I was very much in love.

I found out that sometimes things can be going smooth, and in a moment, everything can change. Have you ever experienced this? Like the Philippine storms — when it rains, it pours. It was announced that Dr. Bill's second term as the medical director was coming to an end. Not only would I have to say goodbye to this long-time mentor and friend, but I would also have to prepare myself for another big change. Upon Dr. Bill's departure, I would be transferred to the radiology department. Moving to x-rays from being the medical director's secretary was a serious demotion. I must tell you that my ego was a little (no...very) hurt. I did not think I could

 Living a life of gratitude, abundance and purpose.

take this new position. I was about to graduate with a degree in commercial science and was already soul-searching when I heard this distressing news. I decided it was time to move on, but how could I accomplish this?

 # Chapter 5

Love — The Glory And The Sorrow

"Love begins with a smile, grows with a kiss, and ends with a tear."
Taken from *Moments*

In the same period when I found out there would be a new medical director of Cardinal Santos Memorial Hospital and that I would be facing a demotion, something else happened that would shake me to the very core of my being. It had to do with my beloved boyfriend, Chris. You know, despite what you might think after reading this, Chris is a very kind and extremely intellectual person. He graduated at the top of his class in one of the best schools in the Philippines. This particular school was either for the very wealthy or the top scholars in the country. His graduation was something to be proud of.

When I first met Chris, he was a seminarian, which means he was studying to be a priest. He came to the hospital periodically because it was one of his apostolic works. It was not hard to notice that he was an avid reader. I would always see him deeply engrossed reading his books. It was in this hospital's charity ward through a friend named Riza that our friendship bloomed. We used to talk whenever time permitted and we often exchanged notes and letters.

 Living a life of gratitude, abundance and purpose.

I was impressed most especially when he sent me poems that he composed. I knew that I could not possibly flirt with him because he was in the process of becoming a priest, but it was certainly difficult to hold back at times — I was developing a strong crush on this seminarian. This non-flirting made our relationship pretty safe, but I knew at some level that I was falling in love with him.

We stayed as close friends for approximately two years before we figured out that our feelings were mutual. Chris was falling in love with me, too. One time, after one of his out-of-town trips doing missionary work, he came back to the hospital and gave me a very special present — a guitar. I was thrilled! It reminded me immediately of Sister Eliza and the wonderful guitar songs that she sang to me at La Concordia College. It was an unbelievably special moment followed by an incredibly sad moment.

As I was receiving that special gift from my friend, he broke some very sad news to me. His mother had just passed away. Understandably, he was completely heartbroken. He was the eldest son and he had three brothers. I remember how he cried his heart out on my shoulder that night. Something else happened which made the whole experience bittersweet for us both. In addition to the sorrowful news about his mother, he revealed something quite shocking — he was getting out of the seminary! It was a time of endings and new beginnings. That night, we grieved over the loss of his mother, and that night we started an amazing romance.

 Living a life of gratitude, abundance and purpose.

We stayed up all night together (not a thought of sleepiness) sharing our deepest thoughts and dreams while walking hand in hand along the shores of Manila Bay. Before daybreak, just as the first pink glow of morning sun was lighting the horizon, we went for breakfast together. I vividly remember that he disappeared for a moment and upon his return he had something hidden behind him — a beautiful, fresh, burning-red rose. That moment is one of the sweetest memories ingrained in my heart. I was in heaven!

I went to work that day completely glowing with joy — still no sleep from the night before. The following evening we would see each other again. And this love affair and routine would go on for a long while. I was so happy for Chris. Starting a new life, everything else fell into place for him. Because of his highly acclaimed background and super intelligence, he instantly got hired in one of the prominent businesses in Manila. One day, he surprised me by saying that he requested to be transferred to a branch closer to the hospital where I worked. I guess he wanted to eat lunch with me every single day. We truly adored each other.

In addition to daily lunches, we would eat dinners together either in a restaurant or in the boarding house where I lived, followed by trips to the movie house. Chris loved to read books and he also liked going to the cinema. We attended countless movies, strolling in and out and always arm in arm. We even took out-of-town trips together. We introduced each other to our families. My mother, for

 Living a life of gratitude, abundance and purpose.

instance, did not particularly like the idea of her daughter going out with an ex-seminarian. For her, it was not right to change vocation. She believed that he should go back to the seminary because, for her, he belonged to the church and not with me. I might have been very obedient during my younger years, but nothing could stop me at that point. I was devotedly in love. This might be one of the first times that I did not go with my mother's wishes. Instead, I followed my very own heart.

Every morning, the first thing we'd do was call each other on the phone. Chris was always my first caller. It is real funny to recall that in the mornings I would double the pace sometimes half running as I would come closer to my office. The phone would be ringing and I would be sure that he was on the other end. In fact, we continued to talk on the phone at least two or more times a day, every day, for three years.

I really do not know what we talked about because we saw each other practically every day and we usually parted ways around eleven o'clock most evenings, unless I had night classes, in which case it was often much later. For sure, those of you who are young and truly passionately in love can easily relate to what I am talking about here. We both shared our deepest feelings with one another. We talked about our dreams, our aspirations and our fears. We were best friends. Does this sound too good to be true? In the end, I guess it was.

 Living a life of gratitude, abundance and purpose.

Breaking Through The Heartbreak

After a sweet three years together, around the time I heard that Dr. Bill was leaving the hospital, something cooled off in my relationship with Chris. Things just didn't seem right. Everything was going so smoothly, and then suddenly it started to break down. Imagine yourself in a very intense relationship. You are inseparable from your beloved, and then out of nowhere you've lost him or her. What's worse, you have no idea why. This was my situation. I had given this relationship my heart and soul, my full trust, and then suddenly it was over. Shortly before Dr. Bill's term was over, I also lost the love of my life, Chris, my first real love. At that time, I didn't understand why our relationship went down the drain.

I felt so betrayed, so cheated and so resentful. I was devastated, shocked and distressed. My heart was shattered. No words can ever explain how deeply I was wounded. If you have been in my shoes, you know what I mean. God knows how much I cried and cried my heart out and for how long. I would be walking along, thinking about our happy moments, and suddenly be overcome by complete sadness. I was envious of the other lovers whom I saw along the streets, in the college and in the hospital. Sweet couples seemed to be everywhere! Tears would flow down my cheeks in the strangest places. I stayed away from the movie houses for a while after our break-up. I could not stand to be reminded of our blissful times there. Actually, I avoided all the familiar places we used to go to.

 Living a life of gratitude, abundance and purpose.

At first I thought this must be the end of the world for me. I kept thinking to myself, over and over again, where did our relationship go wrong? Actually, I have to mention that I believe Chris once told me that he was ready to settle down whenever I was ready. I thought that it was still premature. I felt that the time was not yet right. I had other commitments, primarily to my education and my family, and surely we could wait awhile to get married. Did I make a mistake? Did I wait too long? What did I do to deserve this? How could I go on? How could I pick up the pieces of my shattered heart?

After months of living like a zombie, slowly I began to remember *my* visions, *my* dreams and *my* desires. First and foremost, I was committed to helping my poor parents and my younger brothers and sisters. They needed me. During this lowest period of my life, a few really great supporters, such as my best friends at the time TJ and Pauline, turned up to console me and help me deal with my heartache. They all meant very well. But sometimes nobody can ease the deeply ingrained emotional hurt for you.

The break-up with my first love was the most painful experience I had ever known. I think it was the power of prayer that really got me through. The Divine guided me and I knew that it was time for new beginnings. I simply had to make room for new experiences if I was to survive the pain. This meant saying goodbye to my first love, as well as farewell to Dr. Bill and Cardinal Santos Memorial Hospital.

 Living a life of gratitude, abundance and purpose.

Little did I know, I would soon be saying goodbye to my dear country, the Philippines, too.

Approximately three years later, I sent Chris an invitation to my wedding. I guess I wanted him to know what I was up to. Before my wedding day, I heard that he tried to reach me. We never did connect, but he left a message for me saying that he wouldn't be able to attend the ceremony, but he sent his congratulations. We briefly saw each other six months after the wedding when I returned to the Philippines while waiting for my visa to Canada to be approved. All I remember him saying was that when he heard I was getting married, a heavy load was lifted off his shoulders. I'm not sure what that meant. I showed him the photo of my husband, Ted, and he said that he was happy for me. I did not dare ask about his family then. That was the last I heard of Chris until many, many years later.

In the year 2001, my youngest sister Mary Anne applied for a job in one of the largest corporations in Manila. On the day of her interview, she was led to a big office where she was stunned to find out that her interviewer was none other than Chris. She was barely seven-years-old when I was going out with him, but because she had seen him several times in our tiny house, she remembered him. I wonder if somehow he saw her name among the applicants and he recognized her last name. Perhaps Chris was curious, so he arranged things so that he would be the one to interview her. You might be wondering how that interview went. Well, instead of a

 Living a life of gratitude, abundance and purpose.

business interview, he asked my sister many questions about me. For sure, you guessed it right — she did not get hired, to her obvious disappointment. However, it was not meant to be. Within the next three years, she would actually end up living in Canada with me.

Later in that year 2001, I visited the Philippines for the first time without my family. This was after the tragic events of September 11. Coincidentally, I was about to leave for the airport to catch a flight to the Philippines on the morning of September 11. My circle of friends advised me to indefinitely postpone my trip because worldwide war could be imminent. Upon hearing the word 'war' the more I was homesick to see my family and relatives back in the Philippines. My children would be all right with my husband. He knew I was homesick and that I should go. As soon as the international flights resumed, I did not hesitate any longer. I flew back to my original home sweet home, the Philippines.

My last visit before this one was five long years earlier. My parents, brothers, sisters, nephews and nieces were all very excited to see me, although they constantly asked where my husband and our daughters were. On the first night, it was warm but breezy — the typical tropical climate in Lian, Batangas. We all gathered outside our porch exchanging stories and catching up with the latest family news. My sister Mary Ann told me of her encounter with Chris, and of course I got very excited. It had been many years of not hearing anything about him. I guess that first love never really dies

 Living a life of gratitude, abundance and purpose.

— it occupies a special room somewhere in your heart. Mary Anne handed me his contact number and I sent him a text message, but I did not divulge who I was. My sister Aida helped out in the text messaging. We wrote, "Your old time friend is in town, guess who?" I wanted to play a little guessing game with him. I didn't really want to give a clue that might just give away who I was.

After a few exchanges of text messages, Chris still had no idea who was contacting him. I thought after all these years apart, he must have forgotten about me and therefore I must forget about these silly text messages. I was about to stop altogether when my brother Jose started playing tunes on his keyboard. He played one particular melody — *Don't cry for me Argentina* — what perfect timing! That song used to be one of our favorites. I phoned the number of Chris and let him hear the music on the line. The excitement began to build. Finally, he identified who was on the other end. He wanted to know where I was, when I arrived and how long I would be around — he asked so many questions. He also requested if he could see me during the next day or so. I agreed.

We met two days later. I brought my sister Mary Anne with me to the reunion for support — just in case. The flashbacks were so strong and the emotions were so intense within me. I hoped seeing Chris again after all those years would bring some closure, but it didn't make my nervousness go away. Both of us were already married, but it was hard to let go of old feelings. I must admit, the

 Living a life of gratitude, abundance and purpose.

feelings at that moment were mixed emotions of pain and joy. He brought Mary Anne and me to a very special Filipino restaurant and asked if he could have the pleasure of ordering for us. This was really nice, especially because the years away from the Philippines had caused me to forget what Filipino food I really enjoyed eating.

Chris ordered many dishes. Then he asked me if I noticed anything. I replied that I saw a whole lot of foods, probably too much! He then said that the things he ordered were all my old favorites. He remembered everything I used to love — how sweet of him! My sister mentioned later that she was nearly in tears watching the two of us. It was amazing, but I knew that I had another life now. Our past was wonderful to reminisce, though we could never go back there. I was in love with another man. Chris and I were not meant to be. I showed him recent photos of my family — my husband and my two teenage girls. I wanted to show him that I had built up another life, totally different from before.

After our so-called romantic lunch and reminiscing of the past, Chris invited Mary Anne and me to his office. Wow! I was so impressed. He was now an assistant vice president in this huge corporation. I was so proud of him. He had come a long way. He had his own secretary and his own conference room overlooking the business district. Chris also showed me a photo album of his family. For the very first time, I saw a photo of his wife. She is about three years younger than me and very pretty. She also holds a high

 Living a life of gratitude, abundance and purpose.

position in the business world. They have two good-looking boys and one precious, beautiful girl.

Upon my return to Canada, I told Ted about my meeting with Chris. I told my beloved husband all the details about what happened during the meal at the restaurant. To my surprise, Ted replied, "Honey, he still loves you. Did you mess up marrying me?" I simply said, "Honey, I belong to you." I sent Chris a significant four-page letter, which I had written in the airplane on my way back to Canada. I literally poured out all my old feelings of hurt. I told him about everything that happened in my life after we parted and how thoughts of him would cross my mind every now and then. I also openly told him that I forgave him and I thanked him for all the good memories. I think this was good healing for both of us. Seventeen long years after our break-up, I was able to move on and put things into perspective. I fully understood the circle of life, the circle of true love. I have totally forgiven him. He was very thankful for that moment. I felt so free, so very free.

In March of 2003, Chris finally met my husband and our two daughters. It was a wonderful feeling. My two teenage girls now know of their mother's famous first-love story. If anything at all, I wanted my girls to know that it is wonderful to fall in love, but sometimes it can also be very painful. Ted, my loving husband, knows that Chris had been a special part of my life. He fully understood that. Ted also knows that I married him because I love him entirely.

 Living a life of gratitude, abundance and purpose.

I love my husband for understanding my past. He has never been jealous and is very trusting of my feelings and emotions. I consider myself more than lucky this way. I don't think Chris is keen on introducing us to his family yet. My sincere hope is that perhaps someday he will. That's quite all right with me. I respect that. I know he cared and I know we are both happy with our own families now. What's important is that we got closure by resolving our issues and now we are friends.

VALUABLE LESSONS OF LOVE

Looking back, I now know all the answers why I didn't end up with him — I am named Jhet as in jet plane, I love my family and I also love my travels and life in North America. Chris and I had a great love, but it was never meant to be. This is our destiny, as simple as that. I wish I'd known that before. Don't we all wish that way? It would have saved me from all those tears and deep heartaches. Ted is actually grateful to Chris. He thanked him for leaving me, if you can believe that! Ted said that if Chris hadn't left me, he never would have been able to marry me. True. And there would be no Michelle and Catherine, either. Life would have been totally different. How sweet is my Ted. That's the way life goes. We should always count our blessings.

My dear readers please remember that there is no smooth sailing in life. There will be many ups and many downs. When you reach for the stars, there might be some natural hurdles and obstacles. You may fumble and fall. Be ready to get up, stand firm, and rise to these occasions. I have found that it is not what happens to us that matters most but what we do about it that is really important. When times were tough for me, I simply rested awhile, and then I did my best to keep moving forward, one step at a time. Of course, this is easier said than done at times, but I can honestly tell you that it is the only way to live. Be aware of the adversities throughout your lives. They can be blessings in disguise. God may be trying to teach you through painful experiences.

There will always be solutions for problems and there will always be something else out there for you. I'd like to think that above the clouds of adversity, the stars are still shining. Things in my life didn't always make sense to me, but when I surrendered to the flow, I always found joy again. I have often thought back to my most painful life experiences only to notice that I re-experienced them with a sweet smile on my face. How could I do this? Well, I know now that those hard times made me stronger and taught me the valuable lesson of perseverance. Without those challenges, I would not be the person I am today. I am stronger and feeling more alive because of those setbacks in my life.

Even my own heartbreak turned out to be a blessing in disguise. I have finally admitted the fact that my first love and I had a great love but we were not meant for each other. After many years of

 Living a life of gratitude, abundance and purpose.

pain, I have completely forgiven him and have been able to see the truth of why we broke up. We now have our own families whom we both adore. We have been blessed with incredible happiness and abundance in our own lives. I no longer feel the hurt of our separation. It is amazing how I totally healed myself with the help of a little time, intentions and prayer. Our love was not in vain. We both became stronger and wiser. I thank God each time I think of my first love. I am so grateful that I was able to experience him. I will always cherish the precious moments and wonderful memories, but I know that I am exactly where I need to be now — with my family and with my husband, Ted. This was always my destiny.

When I first wrote my stories for this book, though I wrote with passion and strong emotion, I avoided identifying many of the deeper details. I realized later that you, my readers, deserved the truth and I needed to open my heart and express my inner feelings. I didn't want to cause any hurt. The truth is that Chris was my very first real love. He was an integral part of my life then. I hated him when he left me. Chris caused me so much grief, deep within. But after the years passed, forgiveness came and now all that is left is love again. It is a different kind of love, of course. I decided to share this truth with you because I believe that I have a message for those of you who have fallen in love only to find that it isn't working out.

Some of you, especially the younger generations, might think you'll never get over heartaches. You might even consider hurting yourself because you think the end of your love-relationship means the end of the world for you. I can understand this kind of thinking. It certainly felt like that for me, many times over. I think it took me almost three years to fully recover from my pain. I want you to know, though, that those hurtful moments are but a camouflage for greater things meant to be.

Those painful trials are a vital part of life and learning. You will become emotionally stronger as a result of those trying moments. Most of all, keep in mind that God has something else, something different, perhaps something better, waiting for you down the road. This is what happened to my very colorful love life. Read on and find out how wonderful things got for me. I have only lessons and cherished memories, deep in my heart, which no one can take away from me. No regrets.

 Living a life of gratitude, abundance and purpose.

Living a life of gratitude, abundance and purpose.

HUMBLE BEGINNINGS

2. A typical nipa hut *"bahay kubo"* in Pader, Batangas, my home village.

1. My parents wedding on May 24, 1954.

3. A mini grocery store *"sari-sari"* gifted to my parents from Ted and me for them to be self sufficient.

4. Me at a very tender age, outside the nipa hut where I was born and spent my childhood years. Circa 1962.

5. One of the muddy roads where I used to walk barefooted, to and from school, come rain or sunshine. Circa 2004.

6. "*Kanga*" — a mode of transportation in the rural Philippine countryside and a carabao to pull the load.

7. Just like a "*kanga*" but this cart two wooden wheels.

8. Jeepney — a typical passenger vehicle outside a typical "*sari-sari*" store.

9. Tricycle — a motorcycle with a si car. It can fit half a dozen Filipinos more with a tight squeeze.

10. La Concordia College — managed by the Daughters of Charity.

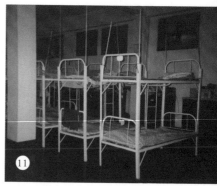

11. My relatively comfy quarters at Concordia where I lived for two yea while attending college.

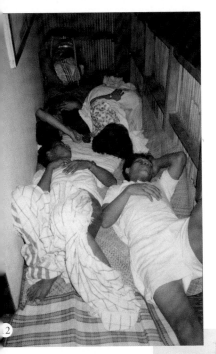

12. My family sleeping like packed sardines, which is a typical situation in a poor Filipino household.

13. Cardinal Santos Medical Center in Manila where I worked for seven years after graduating from La Concordia.

14. Saint Claire Academy where I had my first taste of education as a young child in kindergarten.

15. A wooden statuette sold in tourist shops all over the Philippines — a carbon copy of me from my vending days at Matabungkay Beach.

16. A farewell party with a number of my good friends the day before I left for Yemen in 1984.

YEMEN

2. First time seeing and harvesting from vineyard — ruby-red delicious grapes.

1. My constant companion and me — a special guitar, in Sana'a, Yemen.

3. Typical Yemen landscape I would see looking from my hostel window.

4. Party time at the US Marine House with my buddy Ed Costello. As a child, I used to sell fruits to foreigners, now I socialize with them as friends.

5. After three long years, I found a genuine love again. This time it was for real and Ted and I have now been happily married for eighteen years.

Working in the purchasing department of the [lar]ge American oil company that hired me away [fro]m the Al Thawra Modern General Hospital.

7. Dr. Milos Janicek, Mening and me at one of our parties in Sana'a, Yemen.

8. Looks like I'm buried at the Red Sea shoreline.

DISCOVERY TOYS

1. One of the best things that happened with Discovery Toys, we met our now best friends Tami and Brent Calvert.

2. Wearing our proudest smiles, somewhere in the Caribbean.

THE MANILA HOTEL WEDDING

1. April 8, 1987 — at the luxurious Manila Hotel, Roxas Boulevard, I became Jhet Torcelino-van Ruyven.

2. Eye to eye, heart heart, soul to soul, I g you my love forever.

3. The night before our wedding, dinner at Club Filipino, sponsored by Dr. Bill. With us in the photo are Alice, Dr. Nellie Acosta, Dr. Ernie, Dr. Bill and Dr. Annie Perez. Annie organized our entire wedding.

4. My mother's sweetest kiss of love and pray that touches the bride's heart.

5. Presidential Table — Torcelino-van Ruyven wedding reception.

PHILIPPINE VISIT

1 Ted taking a native shower in the little creek, as I often did as a child.

2. Michelle and Catherine having a wash in unusual bathtubs in the Philippines.

3 Following the Manila Hotel reception, another party, local style, in order for the rest of our relatives and friends. Roasted pig or *"lechon"* is a must for any special gatherings.

4. March 2004, Catherine climbing a coconut tree. She's got some monkey blood from her mother.

5. One of our many visits to Matabungkay Beach. This place held the most humiliating moments of my life, nevertheless it was at this beach where my childhood's innermost dreams began — the rest is history.

6. At the creek where I used to fetch wa[ter,] take a bath, wash clothes manually and [if] there was time left, have a little fun and sw[im] with my brothers and sisters.

7. Quite a steep hill to climb but beauti[ful,] lush vegetation. I consider myself luc[ky] still. During my childhood we were so p[oor] but our living condition was far better th[an] those poor families in the big city slu[ms] all over the Philippines, most especially [in] Manila. It would break your heart to [see] how young people live in the cramped a[nd] unsanitary conditions surrounded [by] garbage dumps and abject poverty.

8. Father Joe Saplala — another heavenly angel in my life.

HOLLAND

1. Ted's mother, Oma, and I in one of those precious moments with my future mother-in-law.

2. Opa, Ted's dad, together wi[th] me at their home.

New Beginnings

2. *Inay* and *Tatay's* visit to Disneyland. This was our childhood dream fulfilled.

3. Bubble bath soak in our Jacuzzi tub with our daughters, the adorable loves of my life.

The first time in my mother and her's life for them to see and touch w, Mt. Baker, Washington, U.S.A.

Michelle and Catherine playing with ay in front of our home sweet home seventeen years.

5. A prosperous and joyful van Ruyven family Christmas in Canada.

6. Sister Eliza, the nun who named me Jhet, in our garden, summer of 2004.

7. Catherine, superman Tom a Michelle, Halloween 2004.

8. Breakthrough breakfast meeting with Filipino Author Susan Romero-Vidal, Derps and myself at the Mandarin Hotel in the Philippines.

9. The aftermath of a frightening accide which somehow I miraculously surviv

10. The 50th Wedding Anniversary of *Inay* and *Tatay*. Twelve children and Twenty-nine grandchildren later, they renew their wedding vows.

11. With Arlene Mitchell, our fabul interior designer, on the top deck of new dream home. Witness the spectac ocean view, just like one of those gra houses at Matabungkay Beach tha used to admire almost four decades a

T. Harv Eker — president of *Peak tentials Training*, one of the fastest owing success training companies in orth America. His teachings and *uantum Leap* programs have been strumental to my personal growth.

2. Robert G. Allen — mentored by Eugenio Lopez, Senior (Filipino billionaire). He is the best selling author of many financial success books, and co-author of *The One Minute Millionaire*. It's my honor to be a member of his *Protégé* program.

Nido R. Qubein — successful author d winner of the highest awards in the ofessional speaking world. He is an tremely successful immigrant.

4. David Bach — best selling author of the *Finish Rich* series: *Start Late, Finish Rich*; *Smart Women, Finish Rich*; *Smart Couples Finish Rich* and *Automatic Millionaire*. David is a good example of a person who is "paying it forward".

5. Ken Blanchard — co-author, best selling book, *The One Minute Manager*®. I love Ken's wit and wisdom.

6. James Malinchak — author a America's hottest young speaker. He is man with a big heart.

7. Ana Gabaldon — international best selling author of the *Outlander* series. I found myself traveling to England and Scotland with my friend Tami after reading her romantic-fiction based on history books, tracing the footsteps of Claire and James. What a romantic couple those fictional characters are. (Ana deserves all the juicy praises.)

8. Mark Victor Hansen — one of t greatest authors and most givi personalities the world has ever know With us is Lisa Nichols, co-author *Chicken Soup for the African Americ Soul*®. A very sweet lady she is indee

9

Dahlynn McKowen — co-author, *icken Soup for the Fishersman's Soul*®. lady with great compassion, she is a ughtful person who relates straight m her heart.

10

10. Doug Wead — an author and the world's greatest speechwriter. I most admire his heart-core messages when he speaks.

1

Tony Jeary — author of *Success eleration* and the world's foremost sentation strategist. I bought his book he Philippines, read it while on board ght back to Vancouver, then a month r I met him face to face in Los Angeles, ifornia. The law of attraction was ainly working here.

12

12. Catherine Coulter — world renowned romance and suspense thriller author whose titles have been on the New York Times best seller list multiple times. Michael Slade — author of nine psycho-thriller novels. I had the privilege of sitting next to him during the luncheon, he is such a great man with a good heart and soul — far different than the characters in his books.

14. JoAnne Rush — contributing edi[tor] of *The Tale Of Juliet*, speaker and visiona[ry] and owner of *What a Rush Productio[ns]*. She is also my marvelous *Success Tra[ining]* coach.

13. James Lee Valentine — *The Man Of Power*. Author of the *Power System*® series books. James mystically appeared in my life. He is a friend, a sounding board, a mentor, and a man on a mission to positively empower the world through *The Empowered Millionaire Organization*. James is also the unwearied editor of this masterpiece, *The Tale Of Juliet*. He truly is a gentleman and a sweetheart.

16. Dr. Denis Waitley — world autho[r] on high-level achievement and perso[nal] excellence. His multiple accolades a[nd] tremendous achievements speak volu[mes] to the greatness of this man.

15. Jack Canfield — co-creator of the *Chicken Soup for the Soul*® series and best selling author of many books, including *The Success Principles*™.

Tom Hopkins — world renowned
~~hor~~ on sales and an international
~~tivational~~ trainer.

18. Nancy Hardin — independent
producer of feature and animated films
and television movies. She has vast
experience as a Hollywood studio
executive, and as a literary agent, and
book and magazine editor in New York.

Adam Ginsberg — the
~~trepreneur's~~ entrepreneur" having
~~ensive~~ business and training
~~erience~~ across many industries. He
attained the *Titanium Power Seller*
~~us~~ — eBay's highest level. Not just a
~~nology~~ marketing wizard, Adam is
an exceptional speaker and trainer.

20. John Kehoe — lecturer and
philanthropist, topping best seller lists
around the world. Author of *Mind Power
into the 21st Century.*

21. Tito & Esther — dearest friends whom I bonded with at the *Guerilla Marketing Business School*.

22. Rob Riopel — one of the *Peak Potentials* trainers. You've come a long ways, Rob. Way to go!

23. Bob Circosta — *Father of the Shopp Channel*. He has appeared in thousa of infomercials, which have sold milli and millions of dollars worth of produ

24. I proudly present the support te of *Digi-Print Graphics Plus* who hel make possible *The Tale Of Juliet*. T went the extra mile to make this happ L-R: Matt, Katy, Greg, (not in the ph are Kerri, Mary Anne, Anna and Jul who all deserve hearty thanks too).

THE TALE OF

JULIET

PART II

Living a life of gratitude, abundance and purpose.

CHAPTER 6

YEMEN — A WHOLE NEW WORLD

"You have to leave the city of your comfort and go into the wilderness of your intuition. What you'll discover will be wonderful. What you'll discover is yourself."

ALAN ALDA

In my last year as the secretary of the medical director of Cardinal Santos Memorial Hospital, a Yemen recruitment agent approached me at work. He wanted to get permission from my boss, Dr. Bill, to openly recruit doctors and nurses from the hospital. Of course, Dr. Bill turned down this agent right away. Obviously, we did not want to lose our best nurses and physicians to this man's agency. The recruitment agent's name was Vic. As he waited to talk to Dr. Bill, I casually joked with him, doing my best to make him feel comfortable. I laughingly asked him if he had an opening for a medical secretary in his organization. At that time, I did not have any thoughts of ever leaving my job — or my country, for that matter. What for? I was very much in love, I had the perfect job and I was at last finishing my higher education. Vic joked back with me about Yemen but also seriously discouraged me from even considering working there. He told me that Yemen was quite an uncivilized country and one of the poorest countries in the world.

 Living a life of gratitude, abundance and purpose.

I completely forgot about Vic and the joke about working in Yemen until a few months later when my whole world was shaken at the foundations. Dr. Bill's term was coming to an end, I was receiving a demotion and the love of my life was leaving me. I didn't know what to do. Lo and behold, I received a call from Vic and he told me about an opening for a medical secretary post in Yemen. Would you believe that Vic said he had a job for me in Yemen right away! I told him that I could not leave until after my graduation from night school and it was still a few weeks away. This was actually a good ploy to buy some time. I knew that I would need more time to decide what to do. I had to consider which was worse — a demotion to the radiology department or working in poverty-stricken Yemen.

While contemplating the idea of going to Yemen, I came across an old issue of the National Geographic magazine. These magazines are full of good facts and information. Dr. Bill subscribed to this magazine so there were always a few copies lying around. One day, I happened to pick up a really old issue that had an article about Yemen in it. I remember how I poured over the entire article, which described how poor the country really was. My heart started to pound and I got goose bumps all over as I looked at the Yemen photos. What was I getting myself into? Yemen seemed even less civilized than the Philippines. Why would I want to go there? Was I just running away from a broken heart? Or was there some Divine purpose to my life that was unfolding at its own pace?

 Living a life of gratitude, abundance and purpose.

The more I thought about Yemen, the more intense my fears grew. I looked at all my options and assessed all my choices. Finally, despite my growing fears, I decided that Yemen was still more attractive than a demotion to the radiology department and living in the Philippines with a shattered heart. I realized that (especially since my beloved Chris was gone from my life), I couldn't stay where I was one moment longer. I needed a change and I needed it fast! Painfully I submitted my resignation letter to Cardinal Santos Memorial Hospital and I called Vic right away. I'll never forget that conversation. I told him I had just resigned from my job, and he told me something miraculous — there was a temporary job opening in his Philippines office. He said that I could work there while waiting for a visa for Yemen. I was ecstatic! I didn't have to be out of a job for a single moment.

I left for Yemen a few weeks after I graduated. I guess it was time in my life for new beginnings and new opportunities. Little did I know that my huge risk would pay off in an equally huge way. The joys waiting for me during the next few years would far outweigh the heartache I had recently endured.

By the way, years after that fateful decision to move to Yemen, I would find out that the man I was destined to marry read that exact same issue of National Geographic that I read — only he was thousands of miles away. He lost his job in the airline industry, and then picked up an advertisement about a job opening in the Middle

 Living a life of gratitude, abundance and purpose.

East — in a country named Yemen. He did some research and came across the National Geographic in the library — the very same issue that I chanced upon among Dr. Bill's collection of magazines. It is interesting to note that the song played during our wedding was *Somewhere Out There*. Worlds apart, at that moment we were wishing upon the same bright stars.

JHET'S FIRST JET

Our jet plane touched down in the city of Sana'a at dawn on a clear April day, it was 1984. Sana'a is the oldest inhabited place in Yemen. Funny, it was literally the dawning of a new life for me, too. I found myself in a totally different world. Everything was foreign, from the attire people wore to the strange and interesting language spoken. Yemen was so far away from my home, so many miles away from the safety of my dear country, the Philippines. I must tell you that this was the farthest I had ever been from home.

At the age of twenty-five, it was also the first time that I had ever been on an airplane. I was so thankful for the preparation of the recruitment manager, Vic Francisco. During our orientation meetings, he reminded us to not expect much from Yemen, at least not much more than what I was used to as a poverty-stricken child. I remember thinking, "Great, two steps forward and three steps back." Vic's words of warning prepared me to some extent — but not entirely.

 Living a life of gratitude, abundance and purpose.

My only consolation at that time was that my salary in Yemen would be a lot higher than the salary I made working at the hospital in the Philippines. Besides, I said that I wanted change, and I was about to get exactly what I asked for. My experience in Yemen would require my full strength combined with a lot of self-sacrifice. Secretly, I wondered if I was up to it. As I adjusted to my new surroundings in Yemen, I often heard the voice of God, "Welcome to Yemen. Make the most of it. You are here for a reason." I vowed to myself that whatever happened, I would make the most of my two years in this country.

Approximately twenty new medical recruits arrived together from the Philippines that day. We were all filled with mixed emotions. Our faces revealed the questions parading through our mind, and our bodies were tense with feelings of apprehension. What in the world had we gotten ourselves into? How would we be able to cope? A strange looking bus driven by a local Yemeni man arrived to take us to our new accommodations. It was odd to see this man wearing traditional Arabian clothing. I noticed two things right away, the pungent aroma he exuded and the ball that protruded from under his cheek. What was he chomping on?

I would later find out that he was engaging in a common custom of the Yemeni. The ball that he was chewing was what the locals call *qat*. *Qat* is a plant with green leaves. Its leaves are usually chewed for long hours with the aim of elevating the mood. Apparently, it can

 Living a life of gratitude, abundance and purpose.

affect the chewer in many different ways, ranging from experiences of joy to depression and worry.

In Yemen, it is a daily ritual for men to sit around in the early afternoon and have a common meal with friends and neighbors, after which they proceed to stuff their mouth with *qat* leaves. They chew this and slowly suck the juice that's released. They continue to put more leaves into their mouth until their cheeks nearly burst. These sessions generally last for a few hours, after which the men go back to their daily routines. *Qat* farming, by the way, is a lucrative business for the Yemeni farmers, growing *qat* mostly on the mountainsides.

Anyway, we boarded the bus with our belongings and were driven to our hostel. Our new home was a plain-looking four-story apartment building. We were assigned two people to a room and told to get settled. It all seemed very strange to me — the sights and sounds, and the smells in particular were quite unusual. There was a male guard assigned to the door downstairs. I didn't feel very safe around him at all. He seemed to leer at all the women as they walked by. I guess Yemeni men were not used to seeing women with their legs bared. Now, I don't want to be too negative, but I was not used to the interesting aroma that this man exuded. Apparently, our customs of showering were different than his. Besides, this guard could hardly speak any English. What if we needed help? How could we communicate?

 Living a life of gratitude, abundance and purpose.

We did not have the freedom to come and go from the hostel as we wished. There was always a strict curfew in effect for both men and women. The authorities felt it was not safe for us to be out and about, and certainly not appropriate for women to be out at all. The women in Yemen dressed so differently from what we were used to wearing in their customary garments. They had absolutely no body parts showing, except their faces and hands. They wore what is called an *abaya*. I was not used to seeing this at all.

We found the Yemeni hospital authorities were very strict with foreigners, Asians in particular. We were only allowed to go to the market once a week, and only in large groups. We could also only travel riding the hospital bus and never on our own. After each workday, we were practically imprisoned inside that hostel. If we did go out, the locals would flock around us and stare. We would later negotiate with the hospital authorities for better in and out access and a much later curfew.

On the first day in Sana'a, we heard a loud speaker coming from all over town, which sounded somewhat like a loud monologue. We were told to get used to it as the sound was a daily occurrence, not once but five times a day! Prayer and recitation of the Koran is an art of daily devotion for a practicing Moslem. The first prayer is at sunrise, again at mid-day, then during the afternoon, once more at sundown, and the final prayer is two hours after nightfall. It was not easy, but I eventually got used to this ritual five times a day.

 Living a life of gratitude, abundance and purpose.

WORKING AT THE AL THAWRA

The first days of work at the Al Thawra Modern General Hospital were very difficult. I was still recuperating from jetlag and still reeling from culture shock as I was introduced to my hospital routines. I counted my blessings, though, that at least I would be working at the most modern hospital in Yemen. There were quite a few 'white' people in this modern hospital. When I heard them speak, however, I was surprised to find their English was as broken as mine. I guess I assumed that all white people spoke English perfectly. I found out that most of these white people were from Eastern European countries like Russia, Czechoslovakia and Hungary. Although I felt ignorant for not knowing there were non-English speaking white people, I also no longer felt inferior. It seemed there were plenty of people who had the same low level of English language skills that I possessed back then.

Looking back, I think I missed the boat a little. Had I made a quicker decision to come to Yemen, I could have been placed in the medical director's office and not where I ended up. But then again, when you see how this tale unfolds, it all worked out for a reason. You see, when I first met Vic back in the Philippines, he said he needed someone to work in the medical director's office right away. I gave up that opportunity waiting for my graduation. Oh well. It was meant to be that I was instead assigned as a secretary in the x-ray department. What a coincidence. Remember my situation back in

 Living a life of gratitude, abundance and purpose.

the Philippines? If I had decided to continue my employment with the hospital there, I would have been assigned as a secretary in the radiology department. I guess there was a lesson I needed to learn, because here I was in pretty much the same situation — just in a different country!

The hospital in Sana'a made a large investment in the best equipment available, and I was privileged to work with two friendly radiologists from Czechoslovakia in a modern x-ray laboratory. They were very pleasant people and totally professional. I developed a special friendship with the younger radiologist named Dr. Janicek. I also became close with his family. Dr. Janicek and I spent many hours at work together. The room we worked in was so quiet, and we tended to try to fill it up with conversation. We learned a lot about each other in those talks. It was through Dr. Janicek that I learned about Czechoslovakia and how people lived there. The country was communist then, which meant that the people were not very free and the conditions were quite poor.

After we got to know each other better, Dr. Janicek confided in me. I was most privileged to hear of his family's plans to defect from their socialist country and seek freedom in the USA. This kind of thing was a very big deal at that time and no one except for me knew of his family's plans. I had to keep it to myself. I remember the month when the Janiceks left for their usual holidays. They were heading back to Czechoslovakia to visit family. I found out shortly

 Living a life of gratitude, abundance and purpose.

after they left that they had actually headed to the United States instead. I had to pretend that I was surprised, but secretly I was thankful they made it. I am so happy for him, his dentist wife and their son. They ended up in Boston, USA, and Dr. Janicek landed a job at Harvard Medical School.

Have you ever heard the saying, "It's a small world"? Well, approximately four years ago, during a trip to Scotland with my girlfriend, Tami, I found myself chatting with an American couple. This couple said they were from Boston, Massachusetts. I immediately thought of Dr. Janicek and his family and mentioned their names. Can you believe this couple happened to know of the Janiceks — they lived in the same neighborhood! This couple didn't have their phone number or address. Though, I guess they didn't know them really well. However, they did tell me that the Janicek's little boy was all grown up now and turned out to be quite athletic. I never did reconnect with the Janiceks, but I think of them fondly now and then. I trust that our paths will cross again someday.

TOUGH TIMES BACK IN THE PHILIPPINES

While still in Yemen, I resigned myself to the fact that regardless of its uncivilized state, Yemen was where I needed to be for the time being. Besides, my parents could really use the money that I earned, so I continued to work at the hospital there. My salary at that time was only two hundred and fifty dollars a month, plus

 Living a life of gratitude, abundance and purpose.

free accommodation. Out of that income, I needed to buy my own food, clothes and any other necessities. Believe it or not, with my previous salary in the Philippines almost doubled by Dr. Bill from his own pocket, this new salary was still far more than the monthly total I was receiving back home. This is perhaps not much based on North American standards. But, sad to say, this is the reality for most Third World citizens. That is why many of us Filipinos hope to get jobs overseas. Most of whatever money was left after buying my basic necessities was sent back to the Philippines to help my parents pay for the food and education of my younger brothers and sisters.

My parents experienced even more tough times while I was in Yemen. A few years before I left the country, they had taken a risk and moved to Manila to start a small bakery. Unfortunately, their hopes of making money out of that bakery business did not work out. They simply couldn't earn enough to support the rest of their growing children. Besides, the living conditions were too cramped in that small rented space they had. Their tiny room of only a few hundred square feet contained a small-size commercial oven, shelving up to the ceiling used for *pandesal* trays, a table for the dough, one bunk bed, a small closet for a few clothes, dishes, pot and pans, and a very small *sari-sari* store (tiny grocery store). You can just imagine a total of nine people who lived, worked, slept and ate, cramped together like sardines. Then, when the oven was turned on, the entire room would naturally feel like a sauna!

 Living a life of gratitude, abundance and purpose.

My younger brother, Rey, became a cigarette vendor in Manila to help supplement the income of my parents. He would buy a few packs of cigarettes, a few menthol candies and a few packs of chewing gum. He hopped from one *jeepney* to another, enticing passengers to buy cigarettes. The *Jeepney* is the Philippine jitney bus based on the US army jeeps used during World War II. In the past sixty years, the *jeepney* has become the most common mode of transport all over the Philippines — the largest ones can carry up to twenty passengers at a time.

It might be interesting for our North American readers to know that cigarettes, candies and gum are sold individually, piece by piece, to cater to low-income people who cannot afford a whole packet. Honestly, I do not understand why many of these people, who have barely enough money for food, still seem to have money to spend on cigarettes though — albeit one stick at a time.

As for my father, he also became a taxi driver at that time, still in Manila. He drove an older taxi with no air-conditioning that was extremely unreliable. He took an afternoon shift so that he could help in baking the bread early each morning. He had to earn a certain quota for his shift. Any money left over after a full tank of gas would be his. There was no consistency in his earnings. On his lucky days he would have perhaps one hundred or more pesos left over (two or three dollars) but sometimes when the taxi broke down he would have nothing.

 Living a life of gratitude, abundance and purpose.

I would hear later on that Rey was able to save up enough money for a bicycle. He figured he would sell more riding his bike as he could move faster following public vehicles. For me that sounded extremely dangerous. I guessed right, as one day he miscalculated his move and had a terrible accident. They thought he would loose his left leg. It was pretty bad. That accident made my parents re-group the family and decide to go back to the Province, where there would be larger spaces with fresh air and a healthier environment for all of them. My remittances from Yemen would significantly help finance their new life back in the Province.

As the third eldest child in our family (well, second really, since my elder sibling died in infancy), I felt responsible to help my parents. This is the mentality we Filipinos have. Sometimes it is good, sometimes not. Some families left behind in the Philippines expect to be helped, to receive a monthly flow of income from their beloved relatives working overseas. I see nothing wrong with this, except for the fact that some of these families become so dependent on the money arriving monthly. I have seen how many Filipinos working abroad sacrificed their whole life to be able to help their families only to find out later that the money they sent back to their families, was not well spent — and certainly not saved.

As difficult as it was, I acknowledged my way of life in Yemen. It was the right place for me at that time in my life. Being in Yemen allowed me to experience the change I needed, while enabling me to help my parents who were financially challenged. I knew the regular monthly remittances that I sent helped them greatly. I was also somewhat distracted from my broken heart. I just had to make Yemen work, one way or another. Even as I worked though, I often dreamed about finding better employment and higher pay. I guess I had a core desire to better myself no matter what situation I was in. I knew there were other opportunities around — I just had to attract one into my life. After only a few months, and although I had two very kind doctors to work with, I became extremely bored in the radiology department. The work was redundant and I desperately yearned for another challenge — something fresh.

For some of the expatriates, who were used to an extravagant free lifestyle in their home countries, being in Yemen was like a detention center, but definitely not so for me. It was a big change in my way of life, culture and environment for sure, but there were also great opportunities to be had. Although some of the western social life was restricted in Yemen, it was there that I was able to really expand my horizon and meet interesting people of many nationalities.

I was asked by a pleasant English lad to take over the typing of a local newsletter catering to the expatriates. My fast typing skills were well-known in the community — they must have seen how I pounded those keys transcribing Dr. Janicek's x-ray results. When I was approached to help type the local newsletter, gladly I accepted the

 Living a life of gratitude, abundance and purpose.

volunteer job and felt that it was an honor for a Filipino like me to be a part of producing a bi-monthly newsletter — *The Ring Road Rag* (named after a road that goes around the city of Sana'a).

Painting The Town Red

I considered myself lucky the day I met the men from the US Embassy Marines. We had been invited to the Marine House for a get-together. I can't remember exactly who invited me or how I got to that party. But I do remember one man I met at that party in particular. His name was Eddie Costello — Ed for short. We hit it off right away and became fast friends. Ed would often come and pick me up from my hostel. He would show up in a huge American Embassy land cruiser, and would always have a Yemeni driver. Off we'd go together to either the American Embassy or to the Marine House.

The Marine House was a venue open for parties. Many expatriates would go there to celebrate, listen to music and socialize. The Embassy was open to all American workers and their friends. It was a really safe place with an outdoor pool. Ed was well over six feet tall — a giant by my standard. He loved to swim at the Embassy, and I loved to keep him company. Now, I did not drink alcohol or smoke, and I did not know how to swim at that time. Ed and I simply hung around and enjoyed each other's company. Our relationship was purely platonic. Besides, the pain of breaking up with my past love was not fully healed yet and I was afraid to fall in love again — with anyone. Anyway, I did not think Ed was looking for a romantic relationship either, just a friendship.

I was so impressed hanging out with Ed, especially at the Marine House or at the fancy American Embassy. Yes, I know it takes very little to impress a girl from a small village in the Philippines, but not all the Filipino ladies got invited to places like this to hang out, listen to music and meet other Americans. Many of my roommates at the hostel stayed in their rooms while I was out socializing. Though Ed did ask me on several occasions to invite some of my friends to their special occasions, like the 4th of July big party bash and lavish turkey dinners at Thanksgiving.

It is important to note that Yemeni women are normally kept separate from Yemeni men. Women could only travel with their husbands and here I was, a single woman, gallivanting with an American man. I would have been in serious trouble with the police (who had guards on many street corners throughout the city) had I not been traveling with Ed inside an embassy car. When you are with an embassy guard in an embassy vehicle, the police don't question you. I felt very safe, well-protected, and very privileged. While others were complaining how Yemen life was too different and so restricted and too lonesome for them, I was having the time of my life and living my life as a single person to the fullest. I felt really good. What a difference in my life. Not too many years ago,

 Living a life of gratitude, abundance and purpose.

I used to sell fruits to foreigners, now here in Yemen I had the opportunity to socialize, mingle and be friends with them. And they showed full respect to me, too. *Thanks, Eddie!*

Despite the difficult environment, I had lots of fond memories of my first year in Yemen. There was great poverty, for sure, but the country also had beauty. Sana'a, where we were stationed, is one of the oldest cities in the world. There is a rich history there. People are very friendly, in their own way. One of my friends named Kaltum, a local laboratory technician educated in England and from a wealthy family, invited us over to her farm one time. It was there that I saw my first vineyard and first apricot orchard, ever. What a beautiful sight — there were delicious ruby-red grapes for miles and miles.

Sometimes, the Filipino men who worked in other companies in Yemen would also invite me out. Most of us women never ran out of invitations on Friday nights, which is a day of rest in the Arab countries. Once in a while, a group of us would get together and team up with some friends. Whoever had the vehicle would pack us in and we'd drive around town together. Sometimes we'd venture further to other famous villages.

I remember a most gentlemanly local guy, whom I called Uncle Amo Najib. He was really nice. He would often offer to drive my friends and me around. Amo Najib was educated in England and had an open mind compared to most of the local Yemeni men. He was very friendly and we really enjoyed each other's company. We'd often have special picnics or climb mountains or go to the Wadidar — a famous landmark in Sana'a. *Wadi* means water. The Wadidar was a natural basin, or rain reservoir. The extra water in this area fed the vegetation, so it was a remarkably lush spot compared to most others in Yemen.

Come to think of it, I met many interesting people in Yemen. The wonderful friends I made helped give me an emotional cushion while I was away from my loved ones. We were all a little homesick, missing our families and home countries but trying our very best to make it work.

MEETING MOTHER TERESA

Yemen is an Arab country — which means there are cultural differences one needs to take into consideration when living and working there. We were warned during our pre-Yemen orientation that there would be no official place for Christian worship or any Christian church at all, for that matter. I had to psych myself up for this fact. Prayer and church had been such an important part of my life and I needed to prepare for this new change in advance. I couldn't imagine two long years without the Holy Mass, so I brought a prayer book and a small Bible with me to Yemen. I hid them really well, packed among my clothes, for fear of getting caught by the airport authorities. I also asked a Belgian priest, who was then a chaplain of

Living a life of gratitude, abundance and purpose.

the hospital I had worked for, to tape-record a Holy Mass for me to bring along. I was sure I'd miss the peaceful rituals and solemn tranquility of church, but with my newly-gathered items I believed I could face the challenge.

To my delight, though, I found out when I got to Yemen that we were able to discreetly practice our own religion after all. This came about through the intervention and help of the Sisters of Charity, a group of nuns founded by Mother Teresa and an Irish Catholic priest. The Sisters of Charity cared for the poorest of the poor — including orphaned and abandoned children in Sana'a. Most of those kids had mental and physical challenges and had no families to support and care for them. The Government of Yemen provided the Sisters with a small communal home where they made available physical and spiritual caring. They often had additional help from expatriate volunteers.

In addition to their work, the Sisters organized a Holy Mass every Sunday and Friday for Christian foreigners like me. It was during these Friday sessions that I was challenged to take on a role I had never known before. I was called to play a guitar to lead the small choir. The regular guitarist and choir leader had left the country unexpectedly and they needed someone to take her place immediately. She was a far better guitarist than I was. I only knew a few guitar chords and was feeling really scared to step up. However, out of necessity, I bravely volunteered to play the guitar and lead that choir

 Living a life of gratitude, abundance and purpose.

during those Friday masses. Once again, despite my fear, I took a risk and stretched myself just a little. That risk would be rewarded in a wonderful way a few months later.

You see, working with the choir put me into a very visible position during the mass, a position that later allowed me to meet one of the greatest spiritual leaders of our time — Mother Teresa. Can you believe it? Looking back, it was one of the highlights of my entire stay in Yemen. Mother Teresa and I met in the very small house of the Sisters of Charity. We choir members were at the front and during the mass we were seated right next to Mother Teresa herself. The whole house was tiny, so you can imagine how close I was to her. It took me a while to realize how incredibly blessed I was to have been in the same small room sitting next to her. I even got to be hugged and touched by her. We are both about the same size, you see. Later on a friend would give me a copy of a photo of Mother Teresa with me. She was an incredible human being, so full of love and compassion. I thank God for having met Mother Teresa.

LIVING A CHARMED LIFE

Shortly after meeting Mother Teresa, strangely enough, another door of opportunity was opened for me. Perhaps I was charmed when I met her and that was what brought my good fortune. As you know, I was working in the radiology department of the Al Thawra at that time. It was there that I happened to meet an Irish

 Living a life of gratitude, abundance and purpose.

doctor named Dr. Slattery. This particular doctor developed a sincere kinship with me. He would often come to my department to get the x-ray results for his patients. He was working for an American oil company. On his regular visits, he often witnessed how Dr. Janicek read the x-ray results while I was seated across the table from him typing. It was my job to use the typewriter to directly record what Dr. Janicek was reading from the x-rays.

Dr. Slattery said he was impressed with my ability to type so fast. He even said he read the acknowledgement they had written about me in *The Ring Road Rag*. He couldn't believe how I could accurately transcribe every complicated medical word that came out of Dr. Janicek's mouth with such ease. He asked me if I would be interested in working for the oil company. I couldn't believe what I was hearing. I had prayed for guidance. My job had become dull, and I secretly hoped for another opportunity to arise. The next thing I knew, this oil company doctor was helping me put together a résumé for a new and exciting position. He introduced me to the head of accounting for the oil company. I was granted an interview — and shortly thereafter, a position was created especially for me. What a whirlwind! In a few short weeks, my life changed completely.

The starting salary they offered me was nine hundred dollars per month. I was ecstatic! If you remember, I was earning only two hundred and fifty dollars at the hospital. What a promotion. I was almost trembling with joy. My whole family would reap the benefits of this reward. The only challenge that I had to face was how to end my two-year contract with the hospital. I had finished just over one year in total. How could I get out of that contract? My fear was what if the hospital administration would refuse to release me? What would I do then? This opportunity was too wondrous to let go, so I took immediate action.

I do believe that where there is a will there is also a way, so I decided to bravely ask my sister Aida to send a telegram to my current employer. The message said that because our parents were trying to immigrate to the USA, I was needed in the Philippines urgently to oversee family assets. Of course, we did not have any assets at that time (remember their bakery business failed and they had to retreat back to the province) and my parents weren't immigrating. This was just a made-up story to help me do whatever it took to get the new job with the oil company. You might be surprised to know that my story actually came true about ten years later with the help of my eldest brother, Ohnie. He was able to sponsor my parents and they were able to immigrate to Guam, an American territory. Would you believe that my mother and father are now US citizens? Little did I know that it would actually manifest in the future — I was only making up the story.

Anyway, I really felt God guiding me and working things out in my favor, time and time again. I did not ask for another job. I was very willing to finish the one I had. However, God presented me with an opportunity and I recognized it. I believe that we all co-create our lives with the Divine. God shows us opportunities, and we take it from there. When an amazing opportunity is presented to you, do what you need to do to make it a reality. Take immediate action. That is how I have gotten thus far in my life.

I had a two-week break before I started my new job with the oil company. I used those two weeks to go back to the Philippines. To my surprise, the oil company even paid for my airline ticket home. Remember Dr. Slattery? He made sure that my new contract included a round-trip plane ticket. I was able to go back home to the Philippines to visit my family and tell them in person about this new God-given job. What a blessing! I could not believe my good fortune.

While home in the Philippines, I was able to do something I had never done before — I became a tourist in my own country. Aside from spending a great deal of time with my family and friends, I took the chance to visit many local places. I was able to enjoy the Philippines in a new and unique way. I experienced for the first time what it was like to have a holiday, a true vacation, enjoying it with some of my greatest friends.

After my short (but sweet) two-week holiday, and just before my return to Yemen, my mother expressed a serious concern to me. She asked if I was ever going to get married or if I was considering it.

 Living a life of gratitude, abundance and purpose.

She said that she was worried I would end up alone in life, bless her heart. I had not fully recovered from the break-up with Chris, even though it had been over two years before, so I brushed off her concern. I said, "Oh well. When the right man comes along, I'll know. If not, I might enter the convent." At one point in time, convent life entered my mind. Despite my dismissive remarks to my mother, deep in my heart I was also wondering when the right person would come along.

 # Chapter 7

Somewhere Out There

"The perfect men and women of our dreams live in our fantasies.
In this life, we have to settle for whoever comes
close — someone not perfect, but real."

Che

I was so thankful for my new employment situation. When I first left the Philippines, I was prepared to experience two long years away from home. I knew it would be challenging, but I was willing to deal with it. You never know how things will turn out. Here I was, a little over one year later, able to visit home for free and spend a joyful time with my family and friends. In addition to this, I had an even more interesting job to return to in Yemen, a job for which I would be compensated generously. Life was very sweet once again.

My return flight to Yemen was much smoother this time around. I had very little apprehension — unlike the first time I flew to Yemen. I knew my living conditions there would be much different this time. I would be on my own and would be freed from the well-guarded hostel where I used to live. My new job opened up big opportunities for me. I could really advance my career, meet new friends and work with people from different walks of life.

 Living a life of gratitude, abundance and purpose.

I was thrilled with my newfound independence! When I arrived back in Yemen, I stayed temporarily with some friends. After dropping my things off at their house, I decided to look around for a new, more permanent residence. In the afternoon of my arrival in Sana'a, I began my search for a new home. During my search, my female friend Mening and I dropped by a place called the Lockheed Compound. There happened to be a barbecue party going on. The compound was a place where many expatriates lived who worked for Lockheed.

There were quite a few men at the barbeque party and I could tell they were on the lookout for ladies. I kept my distance. Among all the people there, I remember seeing a tall, reserved man standing in the corner. He smiled at me, and I smiled back at him. There was something intriguing about him, but I must admit, it was not love at first sight. It seemed like he was more interested (at least at first) with Mening. I guess she had eyes for someone else though. As for me, I was not overly interested in him or in anybody else for that matter. I think I had forgotten how to love in that way.

My previous dating encounters in Yemen had not been well. I had gone out with two men on separate occasions when I was in Yemen before. I thought that these men were sincere in their intentions, but as it turned out, they were not. I discovered that the first man was married and the other man had a fiancée back in his homeland. I can't blame the two men entirely — I did my part to

 Living a life of gratitude, abundance and purpose.

attract them. There is a universal law called the *Law of Attraction*. Have you heard of it? It states: "What you focus on tends to expand." For example, at that time in my life, I was heavily focused on the fact that men were untrustworthy. I really did not think they could be trusted. Lo and behold, I attracted not one, but two untrustworthy men into my life.

Anyway, the tall man whom I saw at the barbeque that day eventually did ask me out — that is, after Mening turned him down. His name was Ted. During our first date, I did most of the talking. I shared my life story with him and was as open as possible. He knew from the very beginning what I was afraid of and what my weaknesses were. I didn't hold back at all. I told him who I really was and exactly where I came from. I figured I might as well tell him everything, in that way, if he wanted to change his mind about me, he could do so right away — and the earlier the better. I really did not give him a chance to tell me about his life at all. Looking back, my little speech did not have the effect that I thought it would have. That is, I didn't scare him off, because he asked me out on a second date.

During that second date, Ted intentionally took me to his home. Maybe he figured that if he couldn't get a word in about himself during our date, at least he could show me something about his world. When we arrived at his place, my eyes immediately scanned the surroundings and I found the evidence that I was looking for —

 Living a life of gratitude, abundance and purpose.

I saw a photograph of a boy who looked exactly like him. My mood changed suddenly. I asked him to take me home right away and I vowed to never see him again. I didn't even want to hear his story. I thought this guy was another liar, a cheater! Here he was dating me, yet he was married and had a son. I was so upset and angry. I knew it — men simply could not be trusted.

It took a week of consistent visits to my office before I would even look at Ted again. He practically stalked me every single day, and I totally ignored him. He would park his car outside and wait until I got off from work, only to see a taxi pulling in and I getting in the taxi as fast as I could. I didn't know what happened next, but at last I gave in when one of his friends told me that he had been divorced for many years. His original marriage lasted for less than two years during which time they had a son. The son was living with Ted's ex-wife in Venezuela. Sheepishly, I decided to give this guy another chance — and he had the courage to ask me out again.

After our next date went smoothly, Ted started visiting me more regularly. We were getting to know each other, albeit slowly. One day, he excitedly announced that he was going home to Holland for a holiday. I was astonished when he asked if I would come along with him to meet his parents. I didn't know what to say. Ted was aware of my past love story and knew that I was having a hard time trusting someone again. He explained to me that he thought I might be able to trust him more easily if I met his family. At first, I did not

 Living a life of gratitude, abundance and purpose.

take his offer very seriously. I was not really prepared to ask my new employer for time off. I had just started working for this company and had just spent two weeks having a holiday in the Philippines.

I wasn't sure that Ted fully understood. I thoroughly loved my new job. My work was stimulating, my boss was great and I really liked the philosophy of the company. My input and suggestions were always welcomed and acknowledged and this was entirely different from any other place in which I had worked. I was content and could not ask for anything more. To ask for a holiday after just one month on the job felt impossible. I decided right away that I would not even try. I respected this company and I was very thankful for the opportunity they had given me. There was no way I would jeopardize this special chance.

The problem was that I had become somewhat fascinated with Ted and was excited by the idea of going to Holland with him. I was also intrigued to hear the real story of his last marriage from his parents, and I was interested to see Holland. What could I do? I prayed for guidance and decided to ask my friends at work. During lunch one day, I shared my situation with my colleagues. I told them of the invitation to Holland and to my dismay they all went bananas. "You should take it," they yelled. "Go for it," they cried, "even if only for the free trip." I told them I was not sure how I felt about Ted and how I did not want to take advantage of his kindness or generosity. They told me that I didn't need to know exactly how I felt right now, that I could simply view this as a free trip and a chance to spend time with a new friend. Oh, they went on and on! The more I listened to them, the more I realized that it was a pretty incredible offer to decline. I was more and more tempted, especially when my colleagues were constantly telling me I was insane if I turned Ted down. I decided to investigate my options a little further.

As you might know, Holland is right next to Belgium. Well, Belgium just happened to be the home of my most trusted spiritual mentor. His name is Father Joe and I met him during my time at Cardinal Santos Memorial Hospital. He is my very dear priest-friend. He was there to give me love and comfort during my heartaches. He was assigned to Belgium while I was in Yemen. I thought a little trip to Holland might be the perfect chance to see him again. Furthermore, I could get Father Joe's opinion of Ted. Maybe he would come to Holland to meet Ted, I thought. It seemed like a good idea, but I still wasn't sure about asking for time off from my new boss. This little detail was soon taken care of, though.

I didn't know it at the time, but Ted happened to be the close tennis-buddy of my new American boss. I guess Ted took the liberty of speaking with his friend on my behalf. He told him about my situation and asked for his help. I had no idea that this conversation was happening. Ted must have really wanted me to come to Holland with him. On the following day, my boss approached me and said, "Jhet, you can go to Holland with Ted. It is just for a few days.

 Living a life of gratitude, abundance and purpose.

Upon your return, the job will be here for you." I couldn't believe this was my life — my boss was giving me permission before I even asked for it! I saw this as the sign it was all right for me to accept Ted's offer.

Hello Holland

We left for Holland in the summer of 1986. Holland is a small, yet fascinating country. It is famous for its canals, tulips, windmills, clogs and cheese. It is also known as the Netherlands, which literally means low countries. It is known to many that one third of the Netherlands was once underwater and almost half of its people live on reclaimed land, which was once part of the sea. It is also the most densely populated country in Europe. Most of its people live in the cities and towns. Very few houses are detached. There are mostly tall buildings, apartments and condominiums. The Dutch people are hospitable and fun loving. What I adore most about them is their love for flowers. Flower-export is one of Holland's prime trades. Almost every home we visited had beautiful freshly cut flowers.

Ted and I were there for ten whole days. Was I lucky or what? Actually, I was in seventh heaven. This guy was really serious about me, but could I trust him? Was I falling in love again and would this love be lasting? One thing I did know for sure was that Ted was a real gentleman. He introduced me to his entire family, who treated

 Living a life of gratitude, abundance and purpose.

me like royalty. For a Filipino like me this special treatment was unexpected. Oma, Ted's mother, was in her late seventies when I met her, a little overweight perhaps, but a fantastic cook.

Oma, which means grandmother in Dutch, was a homemaker dedicated to her husband and family. She was calm and highly intellectual. She came from a family of musicians and was herself a piano teacher. She hummed songs while she did her household tasks. Oma had strong Catholic beliefs. She studied English after Ted went to Canada and made several trips there. She tried her best to share their Dutch heritage and way of living with me. I found their culture so different from mine. However, because Oma had a fairly good command of conversational English, I was able to relate and talk to her.

We would regularly have tea in their well-manicured garden and spent time getting to know each other in their cozy, organized and very clean European kitchen. Oma asked me so many questions and shared with me some of her best memories of Ted. He is their younger child and would always play rough with his only brother Jan. Ted studied in a boarding school somewhere in the northern part of Holland. According to Oma, Ted is a fully practicing Catholic and was a priest-helper or sacristan during his younger days. Ted bravely left home to study in England when he was barely seventeen-years-old, then immigrated to Canada at the age of nineteen. He funded his education while living in Canada and has visited Holland

Living a life of gratitude, abundance and purpose.

regularly once a year ever since. He had a short-lived marriage with a beautiful lady from Venezuela and they have one son.

Opa, Ted's father, was six years older than Oma. Opa means grandfather in Dutch. His family owned a large parcel of farmland, which he and his forefathers had farmed for several generations. He expressed his love for life through his work and through his worship. All throughout, he provided his family with beautiful fresh fruits and vegetables. During the war years, they actively helped to hide Jewish people from the Germans and were very generous in feeding the poor and the hungry. Unlike Oma, Opa knew no English at all. This made communicating with him a little tricky. We did not understand each other. I could tell though that he was very sincere and highly spiritual.

I remember one time, during one of our many visits to Holland, we thought that Opa was dying. I decided to write him a note to let him know how much I admired him, what Ted was like as a husband and father, and how Opa could be so very proud of his family. I asked Ted's niece Monique to translate the letter into Dutch and to read it to him. I was holding his hands as he was listening and lying down on the hospital bed. Tears of joy flowed from his eyes while Monique read to him the Dutch translation of my letter. He got well and lived for another eight years thereafter. Whereas Oma lived to be eighty-nine, Opa died only a few months short of his one hundredth birthday.

 Living a life of gratitude, abundance and purpose.

During my stay in their house, Ted's father would always disappear in the morning. I often wondered where he was going. Curious, I finally asked. I was told that he would go to church early in the morning every day. He attended mass and then would volunteer to clean the church afterwards. I found out that Ted's mother and father were both incredibly religious and had a deep, abiding spiritual faith. On Opa's side, he had three sisters who became nuns and two brothers who entered the priesthood. In fact, between both sides of their family, there were four nuns and four priests. Having parents who were that devoutly Catholic provided Jan and Ted with an immensely strong Christian upbringing. Things were really looking good with this new guy of mine. There was only one more test left to see if Ted was the perfect man for me — Father Joe.

Father Joe and I were very good friends. He knew better than anyone else how deeply hurt I was after my last break-up. When Father Joe learned that I would be in Holland, he took the time to come from Belgium to meet me and talk to Ted and his parents. He knew of Ted's failed marriage and wanted to look out for my best interests. Father Joe really wanted to be able to give his blessings to my new relationship. After spending time chatting with Ted and his family, he was able to do just that, thanks to his gift of languages. He was fluent in the Dutch language and was able to have an excellent conversation with Ted's parents. Before he returned to Belgium, he did not hesitate to give me his approval. He liked and trusted this man and his family. Everything was wonderful. "They

 Living a life of gratitude, abundance and purpose.

are a great family and Ted is for real, listen to your heart, my dear."
Father Joe said.

That trip to Holland was definitely something to remember. I
wondered if these people whom I met in Holland would be my
future in-laws. Was this it? Before I left Yemen, my Filipino colleagues
told me that Holland was famous for fine diamonds. They told me
to make sure that I got one while I was there. They even jokingly
told me to do whatever it took to get one. My finances were not
very good at that time. I had just come back from the Philippines
and had just started a new job. I received my first paycheck before I
left for Holland, but I had already sent most of it to my parents.

One day while Ted and I were strolling in Amsterdam, we passed
by several jewelry stores and Ted actually asked me to pick a diamond
ring. I had a sudden burst of nervousness. I was not one hundred
percent sure if he was serious about me and I was also unsure of
how I felt about him. Everything happened so fast. It seemed like
we had just met and hardly knew each other. I thought it was
impossible to know what my true feelings were when I had only
known this person for one month. He had not even met my family.

So many things whirled through my mind. I remembered how
sincere and direct I had been with this man. He knew exactly how
poor my family was in the Philippines. He knew that a big portion
of my salary went home every month. What would he think if I let

 Living a life of gratitude, abundance and purpose.

him buy me a diamond ring? Would that mean I was submitting to him? Was he trying to buy me by offering me diamonds? Those jewels were very tempting. All I ever had as a child were the fake trinkets sold in the corner stores or at the carnivals. You know, the ones usually encased in a candy wrapper. These diamond rings were far more beautiful than anything I had ever seen before. I started to think quickly now.

Suddenly, I came up with the perfect proposition — at least I thought so. I took him aside to discuss what I wanted to happen. I told him that there was a diamond ring I had my eye on but I wanted to ask him something first — could I pick the ring that I liked even though I did not have enough money to pay for it right then? I told him I would let him pay for the ring as long as he let me pay him monthly installments when we got back to Sana'a. Ted was astonished at this idea of mine. He turned beet red. Maybe he thought this ring was his ticket to my heart and now his plans were ruined. Ted really hesitated at first but soon realized that I was serious about my offer. He acted like it was the craziest idea he had ever heard, but in the end he agreed. I picked the cutest diamond ring I could find. It was just the right size for my thick short finger.

I was going home with so much more than I came to Holland with — trust in my new boyfriend, hope and wonder in my heart, and a cute diamond on my finger! As soon as I got back and received my next paycheck, I paid Ted the first installment for the ring. Up to

 Living a life of gratitude, abundance and purpose.

this point, maybe he thought I was not serious with him. I also sometimes wondered if one of the reasons he was completely glued to me was because he knew I was a very determined person — I could not be bought.

The Wind Beneath My Wings

After our Holland trip we parted at Amsterdam airport. Ted still had a few days holiday left and flew to Venezuela to visit his son. I then went back to Yemen and spent a few days contemplating how I really felt for Ted. It was pretty challenging because every day that he was away a lovely card from him would arrive in the mail. At the same time I knew he was far away visiting his ex-wife and his son. I didn't know if I was jealous or what. It was all mixed emotions.

Well, as the story goes, Ted never let go of me after he returned to Yemen and I didn't mind one bit. We spent hours and hours together sharing our life stories — or mostly mine as Ted is the more quiet type, quite the opposite of me. I told him everything left there was to know about me, including the details of my past relationships and my family's social status. I described the poverty I endured growing up in the Philippines, secretly wondering if it would affect how he felt about me. Would he love me when he truly understood where I came from? I was like a broken record. I even shared my deepest desires and most intimate secrets with Ted. He knew all about my hopes and dreams, my fears and worries —

 Living a life of gratitude, abundance and purpose.

and he loved me anyway! Ted was fully determined to be with me and nothing would shake his love. I was completely myself when I was with him. It was an incredible time in my life — my faith in love was restored.

For weeks after our trip to Holland, Ted and I attended Sunday Mass together and really took our time getting to know each other. I was happy when I was with Ted, and in my own quiet world of prayers, I asked God for a sign. I wanted to be sure. I wanted the Lord to show me that this man was the right one for me. One day, shortly thereafter, Ted announced that some friends were going on holiday and they asked if he could house-sit for two weeks. Ted did not mind being of help to his friends. They were very thankful that he could look after their home, their cats and their flower and vegetable garden while they were away.

During these two weeks I witnessed how Ted dutifully fulfilled his responsibilities looking after their home. This was the time I believe that I really fell in love with him. One day, while watching him water the garden, pet the cats, cook a meal and tidy up the house, I caught myself visualizing my future with him. The only thing missing from my fantasy were two adorable children. These were indescribable feelings. I can still clearly picture those moments. During our whole courtship, I constantly wrote to my dear friend Annie back in the Philippines. I described every last detail of my relationship with Ted in those letters. Once in a while, Annie and

Living a life of gratitude, abundance and purpose.

Ted would even chat on the phone. She was so thrilled for me. I even wrote Derps about Ted and his family, and sent constant updates to Father Joe in Belgium. I had such a supportive group of friends, cheering me on. Of course, I also felt that God was on my side.

Just before Christmas that year, Ted wrote a letter to my parents sharing with them his intentions to marry me. Shortly thereafter, Ted proposed to me, and I gladly accepted. On January 9, 1987, the day of my twenty-eighth birthday, we invited all our good friends for a bigger celebration — our engagement party. Remember the ring? I simply moved it to another finger and without delay stopped paying the installment plan!

After a short and sweet, yet most memorable, courtship, we were married on April 8, 1987 in the Philippines. The ceremony and reception was held at the Manila Hotel. Getting married in a five-star hotel was beyond my wildest dreams. Everything from my wedding dress to Ted's *Barong* (traditional marriage costume for men in the Philippines) were custom made in finest silk. My dear friend Annie assisted in our wedding day. She arranged the hotel reservations, guest invitations and a large reception with a live band. We had menus, cakes, flowers and transportation for our guests. Every single detail was magnificently arranged. Annie was such a great help. She practically planned the entire wedding for us. *Thank you so much Annie!* The wedding was a great success — in spite of a few heart-stopping complications.

 Living a life of gratitude, abundance and purpose.

HITCHES TO GETTING HITCHED

I've never heard of a wedding going off without a hitch. There are always a few things that threaten to collapse the joyous event. Our wedding was no exception. Firstly, Annie had her own last minute details to take care of. Annie was an obstetrician. That is, she delivered babies for a living. A few hours before our wedding, Annie was called to the hospital to perform *two* emergency caesarean sections. Babies have incredible timing! Annie ended up being late for the ceremony — but made it to the reception. I felt blessed that she made it, let alone still full of energy, ready to dance the night away. It was truly a time of new beginnings — and final endings.

A few days before our wedding, something else happened that threatened our well-orchestrated wedding plans. My grandmother died. The wedding day was approaching quickly and there were still so many details to take care of. It would be very difficult for all of us to get away to attend my grandmother's funeral. We only had two weeks in the Philippines. The decision was made that my father would go alone to pay his final respects to his beloved mother.

I understood why he needed to go, but I was upset by the idea that he might miss our wedding. You see, I originally chose to get married in the Philippines for one main reason — so my father could proudly witness the event and openly celebrate one of the best days of his eldest daughter's life. After all the careful planning, I could

Living a life of gratitude, abundance and purpose.

not believe that he might end up missing the whole thing.
Catanduanes, my father's hometown, was just a few hours away by
plane. Everyone assured me he'd make it back in time — but I still
had doubts. He left immediately and we carried on with our wedding
plans, praying he'd return as quickly as possible.

The morning of our wedding, my father called us from
Catanduanes with some disappointing news. He was immobilized.
All flights were full and there was no way he could make it to Manila
in time. This news threw me into an emotional panic. I cried loudly,
threw temper tantrums and even told Ted I did not want to proceed
with the wedding without my father. Looking back, I feel horrible
about my behavior. I was so concerned about myself that I didn't
realize the stress I was putting my husband-to-be under. I mean, I
created real turmoil for him. Can you imagine what he was thinking?
After all the rushing and preparation for a dream wedding in the
Philippines, this little spoilt-child was ready to put everything on
hold. He had never seen me in that situation before. I'm surprised
he did not pull the plug on me.

But Ted proved his love for me once again. I marveled as he
dove into action. In his mind, nothing would stop this wedding.
He looked in the phone book right away and started making calls.
After only a few minutes, Ted had chartered an airplane to bring
my Dad from Catanduanes to Manila just in time for our seven
o'clock wedding at the Manila Hotel that evening. I was shocked

 Living a life of gratitude, abundance and purpose.

and amazed. I did not think these kinds of things were possible. I never thought that a little money and some ingenuity could get someone a private plane on such short notice. This sophisticated man had really fallen for this naive lady. I was beaming.

One of my cousins, who is familiar with Catanduanes, hurriedly boarded this little chartered plane in Manila. Then, on the return trip, the airline company regularly updated us on their estimated arrival time in Manila. It would be close. My father's plane touched down an hour and a half before our wedding was supposed to begin. Things were looking good. At the same time, a beautician was in our room beautifying us ladies. Everything was going smooth and things were buzzing inside this gorgeously decorated bridal room. We were no longer worried about my father, at least he was in the same city now. But there was still one problem — he had to get from the airport to the hotel. Depending on the rush-hour traffic, this could take well over one hour.

My father and my cousin sprinted to a cab as soon as their plane landed. They then discovered traffic on the highway was moving at a snail's pace. It was then that my father and my cousin did something remarkable. As soon as they encountered the heavy traffic, they promptly paid the driver, got out of the taxi, and began to run through the traffic. They weaved in and out of cars, making more progress by foot than they would have done in a car. Each time the traffic started to move faster than they were running, they

Living a life of gratitude, abundance and purpose.

would hop into another taxi. They alternately ran and rode for many miles, finally arriving at the hotel with minutes to spare. In fact, I met my father on the hotel elevator on my way down to the ceremony. Overly excited and in such a rush, he had changed his clothing quickly but forgot he was still wearing his running shoes! *Oh, Tatay. I am so thankful you made it. You did whatever it took to be with me on that special day. I love you so much.*

None of Ted's family attended our wedding. They are such nice people and I am so very lucky to be part of their family. We certainly missed them at the wedding, but despite their absence, the wedding was an occasion to remember for Ted and me. It was also especially memorable for my mother and father. They were so proud to see me get married. Of course, my mother still worried. She didn't know Ted very well, and was still unsure as to how this man would treat her eldest daughter. I knew she needn't worry. I inherited her strong moral character and deep spiritual beliefs. These incredible values helped me choose Ted. I would be just fine with this man.

My father was all smiles that evening. He was truly in awe of the whole event. You must remember that he was a simple family man all his life. To be airlifted on a private plane to attend his first-born daughter's magical wedding at a five-star hotel was exhilarating for him. Each time he looked at me, he was filled with pride. Once a lowly peddler on the beach, I was now a beautiful princess bride. My new exciting life as Jhet Torcelino-van Ruyven had just begun.

 Living a life of gratitude, abundance and purpose.

After our spectacular Philippine wedding and romantic three-day honeymoon in Boracay, Ted and I returned to Yemen to fulfill the six months still remaining on his contract. We continued our adventure in Yemen, now as man and wife, and planned that after six months we would move on to seek a fresh start as a newly-married couple in a new land. I was very sad to leave the company I was with. I worried that I might not find another company that would pay me so well and treat me with such respect. My input was most appreciated by the managers — and I valued that immensely. I had learned so much working for them.

In addition to my work, I had met some really good friends in Yemen. I would miss these kind souls. Some of these people would become friends for life and others would simply drift away. I would have been more than happy to stay in Yemen with those friends, working for that oil company, while sharing my salary with my family back home. However, it was clear that my life direction had changed. I needed to make a move with my new and wonderful husband. It was time to leave Yemen, and time to create a family together. After completing the last six months of Ted's contract, we left Yemen for good. It was truly bitter sweet. We were sad to say goodbye, but eager to share our lives together in a new country — Canada.

 # CHAPTER 8

O' CANADA — NEW COUNTRY, NEW FAMILY

*"It is confidence in our bodies, minds, and spirits that allows us
to keep looking for new adventures, new directions to grow in,
and new lessons to learn — which is what life is all about."*

OPRAH WINFREY

We started the process of preparing for our move to Canada well in advance. The Canadian Embassy required appropriate visas, change of status papers and plenty of other documents. We were careful to prepare everything many months before we left Yemen. That way, it would be ready for us when we were ready to move. It was then we learned that all the important emigration paper work we submitted previously had been misplaced. We were very disappointed with this news.

Leaving Yemen was our chance to say farewell to the land that had become our home and the country where we first met. Our feelings were very mixed not knowing what would be ahead of us. While we were sad to leave our many good friends behind, at the same time we were excited for the new life awaiting us. To help our transition, and to celebrate our new marriage, we booked a two-week second-honeymoon in Kenya. The one we had in Boracay was just too short. We thought an African safari adventure would be perfect for both of us. We were very much looking forward to this trip as our true honeymoon, although it was six months after our wedding.

Our vacation in Kenya was an adventure to remember. When it was over, we flew to Holland where we planned to stay for a month before making our final move to Canada. It was a great chance to get to know Ted's family better. We took the time to visit with Ted's parents and brother. I also met some of Ted's other relatives. None of Ted's family had come to the wedding, so this was a good opportunity for us to make up for that. During our trip to Ted's homeland, I also took the time to visit Father Joe in Belgium as I didn't know when I would get to see him again.

The Netherlands is so different from Yemen and the Philippines. I got to see amazing places like Rotterdam — one of the busiest ports in the world — as well as the famous canals in Amsterdam. Remember how much I love cheese? Well, Holland is the place where they make the world's best Gouda cheese. In addition to visiting these incredible sites, we were also going back and forth to the Canadian Embassy. We had to re-file all of the documents that had gone missing and we were told that my papers would not be processed in time for our flight to Canada. It was official. I could not go with Ted to Canada. I had to either stay in Holland with Ted's family until I got my visa or return home to the Philippines to wait. I was heartbroken. Ted and I would be spending our first Christmas as husband and wife in separate countries. It was not fair.

I decided to return home to the Philippines to wait for my visa. I was warned that this wait could take anywhere from one to six months. I started to think of better ways to cope with my loneliness far away from my new husband. Even though I was around my own family and friends, my life was different now that I was newly married. Contemplating what my new life would be like in Canada, I decided to enroll in an import-export business course and I also enrolled in a cooking class. It was surprising because, although I was now twenty-nine and married, I had never really learned how to cook or bake. Remember, I grew up in a home with no electricity and the most meager amenities. That meant no oven and no baking and only the most basic of meals.

However, I now thought that if I am to be a good wife, at least I should learn how these western people prepared their meals. In short, I kept myself productive while waiting for my travel documents to be processed. Ted and I made many phone calls to one another, and exchanged numerous cards and love letters. These long-distance communications helped build our relationship stronger and allowed us to get to know each other's hearts and minds at a deeper level. In our case, absence did make the heart grow fonder. Ted was able to settle down and re-group himself and find a new job. I do vividly remember one phone call with Ted. He called to tell me that he had just bought an automobile that would remind him of me every day. I did not know much about cars, so when he asked me to guess what it was, of course I had no clue. It was a Volkswagen *Jetta* — how sweet!

THE LAND OF GREAT OPPORTUNITY

On February 7, 1988, after three months of waiting for my visa in the Philippines, I boarded a plane for Canada. Finally, I was headed to my new country and my new husband. I flew via Holland and then on to Calgary, which was my first point of entry into Canada. It was neat because Calgary was hosting the Winter Olympic Games that year. The plane I was on was filled with Dutch athletes traveling to their Olympic competitions. Imagine how excited they were! From Calgary, I continued on to Vancouver. When my plane touched down at Vancouver International Airport, I was reunited once again with my darling husband Ted.

I'll never forget that day. There was snow on the ground in Vancouver — snow! This was the first time I had ever seen or touched the white magical substance. I felt like a child again, picking up balls of snow and holding them in my hand until they melted. I completely forgot about the cold. I simply could not believe how soft and pure and white the snow was. I knew this day was a new beginning for me — the start of a new life of gratitude, abundance and purpose.

 Living a life of gratitude, abundance and purpose.

I must tell you that Canada is the land of great opportunity. It is one of the most beautiful countries in the world, and an absolutely heavenly place in which to live and raise children. There are vast tracks of open land, rich with natural resources. There are the majestic Rocky Mountains covered in evergreens, and dotted with pristine lakes and deep green valleys. Canada has breathtaking views, miles and miles of forest slopes, luscious farms, ranchlands, orchards, rivers, lakes and never ending lush greeneries. It is God's country at its most awesome.

NEW FRIENDS AND WONDERFUL NEIGHBORS

Ted and I settled in a place outside of Vancouver called Surrey, British Columbia. Ted had to return to work shortly after I arrived in Canada. So, I was left all alone in our one-bedroom apartment with little to do. I started to feel very lonely. While Ted worked, I waited for his homecoming. There was a telephone, yet here I was with not a soul to talk to. Life was very quiet here. I spent my time alternately watching TV and reading books and magazines. Ted introduced me to some very nice friends, and they were all wonderful people, but I had just met them and was too shy to call them just to chat. Later, I would make many wonderful friends, but during those early days in Canada, at times I felt very lonely indeed.

We originally planned to have our first home in Canada custom-built, but changed our minds when we came across a warm and cozy Tudor-style home in a nice neighborhood. We decided to purchase the house at once. In hindsight, it was an excellent move. We had heard nightmares from people we met about the troubles with building your own home — especially for someone like me who knew nothing about the endeavor. There would have been so many decisions to be made about appliances, kitchen decor, floor plans and overall design. Remember, the homes I was most familiar with were *nipa* huts whose floors, walls and roofs were made of the fronds of the *nipa* palm. Our first home in Canada was situated in a cul-de-sac in an excellent neighborhood with a view of the ocean in the distance. This was the place we planted our roots for the next seventeen years.

Ted and I were blessed with good neighbors in Surrey. They welcomed our diverse ethnic backgrounds. Later on, when our two daughters were growing up, age-wise there was a good balance in our neighborhood. In addition to us, there were another two young families with children. There were also some retired couples, who became grandparent-like figures for our young children. It was such a blessing that we three newly-married couples started our families at the same time. It seemed that we wives all got pregnant at regular intervals, which made it very exciting.

People in our neighborhood would look forward to guessing what gender the next baby would be. After each birth, the neighbors would tie pink bows in the trees in front of the new mother's house.

 Living a life of gratitude, abundance and purpose.

Interestingly, our three families each had two beautiful girls. How fun! You can imagine six young girls playing around our cul-de-sac — giggling, screaming, riding their bikes, jumping rope, selling lemonade, baking cookies, throwing snow balls, making snowmen and attending each other's birthday parties. Our six girls had such a wonderful time growing up together — an entire world of difference away from my own childhood days.

Two New Angels

A few weeks after our arrival in Canada, a nice doctor confirmed that I was pregnant. Our new life was unfolding quickly. Our darling daughter Michelle Christine came into this world at Halloween in 1988. I was eagerly anticipating my first Halloween festivities in Canada. I observed how commercialized the season was in this country. There were tons of chocolates and candies on sale around the stores and in the malls. I decided to buy several bags of assorted candies hoping to give out treats to the costumed boys and girls later that evening. Once again, the Divine had other plans for me. During the morning of October 31, I began to feel contractions. I called Ted at his place of work and he immediately came home to drive me to the hospital.

I was in hard labor all day, trying my best to give birth naturally. At the last minute, my precious Michelle turned upside down and the doctors informed me they needed to deliver her by caesarean section. On the evening of October 31, 1988, we were gifted with the best Halloween treat ever, a seven-pound, healthy baby girl. Being a new mother was quite an adjustment for me. I had hardly recovered from the shock of being a mother when I found myself pregnant again. Within one year of Michelle's birth, there was another baby growing inside me. Catherine Maria followed her sister into this world just over nineteen months later.

With Catherine, I again tried to give birth naturally. I wanted to avoid another caesarean section. I was in labor for over fourteen hours and everything was looking good — until the medical team noticed that the baby's heart was beating with an irregular rhythm. Suddenly, the baby appeared to be in distress! The doctors decided to perform an emergency caesarean section — *immediately*. They discovered later that the umbilical cord was wrapped around her neck. I thank God she survived. Thanks to advanced technology, too — what a miracle!

Catherine was born during the early morning of June 7, 1990. She was also a very healthy baby. We were told by a lot of people that my belly looked like I would have a baby boy. We took this to heart and were not prepared to name another girl. I had been saving the name Jonathan Nicholas from even before Michelle was born. This time I was really ready. You can imagine my surprise when our baby turned out to be a girl. We decided right there to name her after her very sweet and very caring doctor.

 Living a life of gratitude, abundance and purpose.

I was now the very proud (and very scared) mother of two little girls. While I was pregnant with Catherine I was extremely anxious and always watchful of other mothers with two young children. Was I ever frightened! How was I going to cope? How could I look after not one, but two little babies? They were entirely too close together. How would I manage? Michelle was already a handful. Ted and I did not have a maid or a family member that could assist us with the raising of our daughters. I wondered just how I was going to cope.

Even though Michelle was born when I was in my late twenties, I can honestly say I was not prepared to be a mother. First of all, my own mother never really taught me how to nurture a child. She was too busy making us — one after the other. Remember, my mother had twelve children in all. Secondly, I was a new parent in a foreign country, with a culture completely different from what I was used to. Thirdly, with no family here to help me out during the early stages of parenthood, and with Ted very busy at his work, I would have to handle almost everything alone. I was extremely worried and I attracted the exact conditions to match my negative belief.

To begin with, Michelle had so many allergies and was an extremely sickly baby. She didn't sleep through the night for many, many months. People told me it would get better and that she would sleep peacefully after about three months. Well, that never happened. Even after Catherine was born nineteen months later, Michelle was still not sleeping through the night. One of our friends even suggested we let her sleep alone and just keep a baby monitor next to her crib. Well, that did not last long because she just woke up and fussed loudly every hour. We heard this on the monitor and Ted or I would have to get up and rock her back to sleep. Michelle would wake up so early every morning, ready for more attention. Ted and I were like zombies! For a long while, my life was entirely devoted to Michelle. She demanded so much attention and care. Ted would come home from work, and there would be no dinner prepared. I don't know where the hours went. Thank goodness he was very understanding. My loving husband would immediately take over and play with the baby so I could have a break.

Michelle became very allergic to dairy products, and she developed serious eczema and asthma early in her life. She was very sensitive to dust and also to animal dander. In spite of these afflictions, it was sheer joy to watch her grow. She was surprisingly strong, crawling well ahead of her peer group and walking when she was only nine-months-old. My one saving grace was that I belonged to a dedicated group of mothers. We met during our pre-natal class and continued to meet and keep in touch after our babies were born. We often took turns hosting mom and baby get-togethers where we shared cookies and participated in diaper-changing marathons with one another. More importantly, we shared our personal stories and supported each other emotionally. That group was one of the best gifts I had during early motherhood in Canada.

 Living a life of gratitude, abundance and purpose.

Outside our mothering group, I was often mistaken for Michelle's nanny. Michelle was fair with blond hair and I was dark skinned with dark hair. Sometimes my ego would get in the way and I would snap back, "Excuse me! She is *my* daughter. I am *not* her nanny!" After a while, I adjusted to the comments, and they really didn't bother me at all.

We were lucky to live very close to an elementary school. It was just a block away. When Michelle was in kindergarten, I would often walk her to school with Catherine in the stroller. One day, a teacher (who didn't seem very friendly to me) approached me on the school property. She was holding a sealed envelope, which she handed to me. Calmly, she looked straight into my eyes and said, "This contains a very important message. Could you please make sure that Michelle's mother gets it?" With equally strong conviction and looking directly back into her eyes, I told that teacher that I was Michelle's mother. Did she ever turn red! She was truly embarrassed. After that incident, that teacher found it very difficult to look at me straight. Whenever I saw her, she either looked away or forced a smile and quickly went in the other direction. Oh well, that was an encounter to remember.

Catherine was a very different baby from Michelle. Catherine was a rather delicate, utterly sweet little girl. Thankfully, she slept through the night the first day home and stayed a good sleeper for as long as I can remember. She used to curl up in my arms beside me and when it was time for her to go to sleep she would be out like a light within minutes. Even now that she is in her early teens, she can sleep soundly in most environments. From the very beginning, she was a calm and loving baby.

EASY MONEY

Shortly after Michelle was born, my dear husband decided to buy me a computer and a printer. Having known me as a bit of a workaholic when he was dating me, perhaps he knew that I was somewhat bored at home. After a few days of practice at the keyboard, I needed some additional motivation. That is, I needed an extra incentive to keep me interested in learning and practicing further. I was alone with Michelle most of the time and craved additional stimulation anyway. That was when the entrepreneurial spirit in me kicked into high gear. It had been a long time since I was an entrepreneurial fruit vendor on the sun-swept beaches of the Philippines — but the spirit within never dies, I guess.

I decided to put an ad in the local newspaper advertising a typing service. It was a brave move considering the circumstances. Shortly after putting the ad in, I was contacted by a potential client. My first caller was a gentleman wanting to have his résumé typed right away. I figured I could do his two-page résumé in about an hour while Michelle was asleep. I gave him our home address and instructed him to come over to my house promptly at ten o'clock

Living a life of gratitude, abundance and purpose.

the following morning — right when Michelle would be napping. I also instructed him not to ring the doorbell.

I excitedly watched for his car and leapt up as soon as I saw him pull into our driveway. Unfortunately, I wasn't fast enough. He beat me to the door and rang the bell — I guess he forgot my earlier instructions. The shrill doorbell was like a lightening bolt to the ears of my now startled baby, who immediately started crying. I was so embarrassed! There goes earning my first dollars, I thought. As I let him into the house, I told him I didn't think I could do the job now as I first had to look after my crying baby.

The man was very calm and compassionate, though. He took pity on this little Filipino lady. He waited patiently as I calmed the baby down. He even offered to hold her and play with her while I did the typing. It seemed like a decent idea to me, and less than one hour later, I had finished his résumé. I was not sure if I should charge him, though. After all, he babysat my daughter the whole time I was typing. I handed over his newly-typed résumé and he handed me twenty-five dollars! You should have seen the huge smile on my face. It was the first money I ever earned in Canada — and it was easy!

Some people might be surprised with my entrepreneurial daring. I mean, I did let a total stranger come into my house and I trusted him with my baby. In hindsight, it does seem a little crazy.

 Living a life of gratitude, abundance and purpose.

However, I did what I did — and that man was the first of many customers. After that first taste of Canadian income, I knew I was living in a new land of opportunity. It also confirmed my belief that there would always be a way to make money if I wanted to. When my husband came home that evening, I was beaming with joy. I bragged about the twenty-five dollars that I earned and marveled at how easy it had been. He had a sweet smile on his face — he was so proud of his enterprising wife.

I was now more motivated than ever to continue on with my home-based typing business and eventually expanded it. In addition to typing projects, I also taught tutorials on basic word processing. I found so much joy doing something worthwhile for other people — in exchange for dollars of course! In addition to paying my regular rate, many of my customers would also leave me tips. I felt so blessed. By the time I was ready to give birth to Catherine (she decided to arrive three weeks early), I had a good little business going. I even had to cancel five students, who were scheduled for tutoring sessions, in order to go to the hospital to give birth.

Looking back, I wonder how I ever did it. I had a very young, very needy baby in Michelle, and I was so very pregnant with Catherine. Oh well, I guess I did whatever it took. I feel it is important to tell you that I earned enough money from that little home business to buy us a fax machine, a piano and a pine bedroom set for Michelle's room. I also saved enough for a small savings

 Living a life of gratitude, abundance and purpose.

account and a shopping spree once in a while! Ted's little investment in a computer and printer just to keep me from boredom (he thought) more than paid off. I really should credit my dear husband here. He was always there for me and always supported me in my business ventures. Even though I did not have to work (he provided very well for our family), Ted knew I needed to work. He knew I would not be content solely as a homemaker. I was at my most joyful when I had many different things going on — and Ted respected that.

I remember how those busy days would go. I'd prepare dinner well ahead of time, usually while the girls were having their naps. As Ted got home we'd briefly hug and kiss and eat a quick dinner together. Then, shortly after dinner, I'd be off to my desk to work on my little part-time business. Ted would take care of the girls while I worked. We were a good husband and wife team. Life was busy, but that was what made it so interesting for me.

I continued my typing services for two and a half years until a neighbor complained that the computerized paper sign by our window faced her living room across the street, and was becoming an eyesore. She called the bylaw officer who later forced me to take down the sign and close my little business. To her defense, our home was located in a very good neighborhood, which I later learned was not zoned for business purposes. But there really weren't that very many people coming and going and I must admit I was slightly

 Living a life of gratitude, abundance and purpose.

bitter about having to take the sign down. At the time, I felt really betrayed by this neighbor. Of course, I have since forgiven her for the whole thing.

The forced closing of my secretarial service prompted me to start pursuing other business ventures. It had already crossed my mind that I needed a different challenge — something altogether larger and more meaningful. Typing all day long in front of the computer, although I was compensated very well, no longer held any great excitement for me. It is time to move on and spread my wings a little bit more. So, out of this apparent misfortune came even greater fortune. I accepted the situation and decided I would utilize it to my best advantage.

 Living a life of gratitude, abundance and purpose.

CHAPTER 9

ON WINGS OF DISCOVERY

"Whatever you vividly imagine, ardently desire, sincerely believe and enthusiastically act upon must inevitably come to pass."
PAUL J. MEYER

Not long after I was forced to shut down my home-based secretarial services business, I came across a direct marketing toy company that carried a full line of educational toys, books and games. The company was called Discovery Toys. My two girls had just started pre-school when I became interested in this toy venture. The company had a full line of products that seemed to have immense educational value for children. Initially, I decided to join the company just to get the toys at the wholesale price.

I thought Catherine and Michelle could truly benefit from these products and I didn't see anything wrong with trying to get them at a discount. However, after a few meetings with the company representatives, I became more and more interested in actually selling these toys to other people. You see, the company offered incredible sales incentives. The one particular sales incentive that initially triggered my enthusiasm and got me most excited was an all-expenses-paid Caribbean cruise for two. The sales people who

 Living a life of gratitude, abundance and purpose.

fulfilled the required number of sales for a distinct period of time would earn this trip.

Now, the required number of sales was extremely high — and at first seemed impossible to reach. However, despite those early feelings of fear, my intuition kept telling me I was up to the challenge. The major problem was that I really did not know a lot of people (potential customers) yet. But I was magnetized with the idea of the trip. I was so blessed to have such a supportive husband and this trip would be my gift to him. Besides that, Ted and I had never been on a cruise before and we had not gone on a holiday together since the birth of our daughters. Although part of me did not really like the idea of leaving our two young girls behind, I knew this would be the perfect romantic break for both of us. Before I knew it, I found myself feeling fully determined to do whatever it took to earn that incentive trip. I was about to step outside my comfort zone and learn about goal setting, motivation and direct sales.

Once I established the goal to do whatever I must to make the dream Caribbean cruise a reality, everything else seemed to fall into place. On our fridge, I posted the glossy colored brochure showing a luxurious cruise ship floating over the sparkling blue ocean. It looked very inviting, and very real. I vowed in public to attend every sales team meeting and follow through with every recommended marketing strategy. I started listing all the people I knew, both friends and acquaintances. I kept a keen eye on those

 Living a life of gratitude, abundance and purpose.

people who had children. I brought company brochures with me wherever I went with my girls. Whenever I socialized with other parents, I would take the time to introduce what I did and how they might also enjoy the benefits of the toys.

I learned and taught other parents how simple colored measuring cups could teach young children about math, and how stacking those same cups would teach them eye-hand coordination. I showed them how building blocks and puzzles would enhance their child's thinking skills. I really believed in the products — and thoroughly enjoyed empowering other stay-at-home mothers. This was one of the main keys to my success with Discovery Toys. When we truly believe in the product or service we are selling, everything else works out. Keep this in mind if you are looking to get involved in direct sales. It is also so important to have support. I was lucky to have Tracey Harris to work with — one of the top marketing directors. I also had a ton of supplemental information in the form of brochures and videos, which contributed to my knowledge of the products and how to sell them.

I watched those marketing and instructional videos over and over to learn the skills of toy demonstration. This wasn't an easy task because the videos were in English and that was my second language. I watched them again and again. I knew I'd have to speak English in front of total strangers, so I thought I'd better get more proficient in the language. To gain even more confidence, I tagged along to almost every big event with Tracey. I wanted to learn from a professional — and Tracey gladly took me under her wings. When I first joined the company, I had never driven outside of our little neighborhood. I was frightened of driving in downtown Vancouver on my own, and had never even driven in the dark. I conquered all those fears in pursuit of my goal. Whenever I felt scared, all I needed to do was look at that picture of the cruise ship on our fridge. It seemed to shout at me: *You will be on board this ship!*

During this exciting time, I was very lucky to attract some amazing people into my life. I found myself in the midst of an incredible group of ladies with such diverse backgrounds. But even though we had such dissimilar histories, we all held the common interest of wanting to make a difference in the lives of children. We wanted to make the world a better place through educating children while they played. We were committed to Discovery Toys because we saw how their products worked, and we were dedicated to sharing the wonderful knowledge we had gained.

The sales work was challenging, and the company goals were lofty, but I gained so much through my experiences. I learned how to pace myself and I learned that success comes one step at a time. In spite of my broken English, I was able to recruit a large number of remarkable women into my personal sales group. It wasn't long before I was having team motivational meetings regularly in my home. I scouted the newspapers for educational events for kids and

 Living a life of gratitude, abundance and purpose.

tried to book as many toy demonstrations as I could. I teamed up with Tracey and we went to almost every teacher educational conference and event we could find. If there were parents and children there, Tracey and I would also be there. I was a driven woman with my eye on my goal.

Roadblocks Ahead

One drizzling Saturday morning after enjoying a delicious *panakoek* (Dutch pancake) routinely prepared by Ted, I kissed my family goodbye and started the car. I was on my way to a school event, where I was supposed to set up a play area to sell toys. Unfortunately an unforeseen event happened before I made it to the school that day. I did not see or hear the accident — the only thing I remembered was the siren of the ambulance. I awoke inside the ambulance to a battery of questions: what was my name, what day was it, did I have any family? I remember telling the questioners that I had a husband and two daughters.

The next time I woke up, I was inside an emergency room. Ted was there by my side and looked very worried. He was holding my hands and told me everything would be all right. I was crying and felt very upset. I immediately asked him about our girls. At that point, I was still dazed and I did not know what had happened. I was to be told later that as I was turning left from the middle lane, a jeep traveling from behind smashed into the driver's side of my

 Living a life of gratitude, abundance and purpose.

car. It was a miracle that I survived the accident. The eight-month-old Mazda MPV that I was driving was completely wrecked. God knows how I got away with only a small, six-stitch laceration on top of my head.

It could have been much, much worse. I was told that I narrowly escaped death that day. I thank God for giving me another chance. The thought of dying and leaving my husband and young children behind gives me a shiver along my spine. As you can imagine, that accident shook me up quite a bit, but not enough to put my life (or my dreams) on hold. At first I thought God was giving me a warning sign, but now I know it was actually just my courage and strength being tested that day. I know I was pushing myself to the limit. I would be up late at night and using every free moment to take care of customer orders, shipping toys and coaching my growing number of team members. After the accident, I got myself together and got back to my goal of getting on board that cruise ship.

Back to full-time work just two weeks after the accident, I figured that if I really wanted to attain this goal, I had to expand my horizons. Aside from toys, we also carried books, tapes and educational computer games. I started cold calling on school principals and teachers, school nurseries and libraries, and all the educators that I could think of. I was turned down many times. At first I took it personally. I blamed it on my accent and my inability to explain the products well enough for people to understand their tremendous

 Living a life of gratitude, abundance and purpose.

value. My self-blame continued until such time that I learned how to cope with those defeating moments. Later, when someone rejected my offer, I did not take it personally — I simply moved on until I got a solid yes.

Christmas was approaching and we were told that some companies hosted parties for their employees and children. I thought this was a wonderful opportunity, so I grabbed the telephone directory and randomly called several companies. Well, much to my chagrin, I did not have much luck on this one. I called perhaps two dozen companies, yet I did not get a single yes response from any of them. I thought that I should perhaps give up on this idea. Then I remembered that the year before, we were invited to the Christmas party of Ted's union and they gave away some goodies to the children.

Wow, that turned out to be one of the best ideas I ever had. It took great effort and much perseverance to get to the head of purchasing, but this person said yes to my proposal. I was not able to sleep the night before I was to do a presentation in front of a dozen decision makers in one of the unions of the largest airline fleet in Canada. I prepared by watching the instructional videos over and over again. I carefully selected the products that I would bring to the demonstration. I chose my best looking clothes. And off I went, with the picture of the Caribbean cruise in the front of my mind.

 Living a life of gratitude, abundance and purpose.

The rest is history, as they say. That day I got enough orders to seal the trip for Ted and me. You see, I became very creative and left them no room to refuse my incredible proposal. Not only did I offer to select the most appropriate toys for the age groups of the children, but I would also wrap each present individually, label them accordingly with the names of the children *and* deliver them on the day of the Christmas party. They had nothing to lose. All they needed to do is place the order and I would take care of the rest. I made it appear so easy for them that it was a no-brainer not to place an order with me. I had presented them with all the benefits of the toys and added a lot more value with my personalized service. I still didn't know up to that point where I was going to store those toys and how long it would take me to wrap them all — but I was sure I could figure that out.

Well, the order was processed and got delivered to our house. We had to clear our two-car garage plus our family room to accommodate all the toys. I bought heaps of wrapping paper and ribbons. My good friend Rachel Klause was there to help me wrap the toys individually. Our family room became the scene of what you'd call Santa's Workshop. By the day of the Christmas party we had all the presents wrapped and I delivered everything on time. This corporate order would help us get the trip. With the number of sales I had secured, and with the help of my incredible team, I totally surprised many people by earning that Caribbean cruise. After all I had been through, I was ready for a break.

 Living a life of gratitude, abundance and purpose.

The Discovery Dream Cruise

The all-expenses-paid cruise was indeed the trip of a lifetime and a marvelous dream come true. When I told Ted that I had completed the requirements for the trip he was ecstatic and so proud of his high-flying wife. I was jumping with such joy that I could give something very special to Ted. Both of us had never been on a cruise before, so this trip was very precious to us. It was also the fact that I earned the cruise through my sheer hard work and perseverance. I was very proud of my achievement. That trip represented so much to me. Not only was I excited that we didn't have to pay a penny for the trip, but the cruise was also a tangible reminder that when I used my fullest potential, and did whatever it took, I could succeed.

We were joined on the cruise by educational consultants from all over the world. Remarkably, I was one of very few people representing the province of British Columbia. This was another feather in my cap. The crew treated us magnificently — it was first-class all the way. We attended exciting shows and were granted admittance to the exclusive parties for the 'excellent achievers' in the company. There were all kinds of last minute surprises and perks. The company planned amazing and exotic adventures at each port, and rewarded us every evening with special surprises waiting inside our first-class cabins. I was even recognized on stage as one of the top five in personal sales amongst the thousands of women in

 Living a life of gratitude, abundance and purpose.

Discovery Toys nationwide. It was such a fulfilling moment. It felt really fabulous to be able to give this gift to my loving and supportive husband. I realized that no goal was too big when you truly set your mind to achieving it.

That cruise was just the first of the many wonderful trips and perks I achieved working with Discovery Toys. The next big incentive award I earned was a trip to San Diego, where we stayed at the Hotel del Coronado, one of the oldest and most exotic five-star hotels in the world. This time we took our daughters with us. We were once again treated like royalty. It was so special to take this trip with our whole family. The girls had so much fun with the Discovery Toys people. We ate gourmet meals, attended open bar galas and were invited to wild parties (without the girls of course). We went sightseeing, toured around the city, watched lavish fireworks and enjoyed many other wonderful surprises. Discovery Toys really knew how to take care of us.

I continued to be a stay-at-home mother while working with Discovery Toys for a further two fabulous years. Nurturing myself and my children, whilst teaching other parents and teachers the value of educating children through our products, made for a very full life. I was able to earn many more incentive awards through that company. Including all-expenses-paid trips to Toronto, San Francisco, Phoenix and Los Angeles, and we stayed in five-star hotels in each of those cities. My life was very full.

 Living a life of gratitude, abundance and purpose.

Expensive Business Lessons

It was now November 1995, Catherine was in pre-school and Michelle had just started elementary school. I had been selling toys for almost three years and was starting to crave something new. I began to search around for fresh business opportunities. I thought of becoming a franchisee and seriously investigated one particular business. There was already a system in place and it would have been an easy transition, but I really wanted to be independent. Besides, the franchise required a lot of money up front and I didn't want to start my business heavily in debt. I decided to keep looking.

I came across an office supplies store that was for sale close to the area where we lived. The business was not doing very well, and the couple that owned it wanted to sell the whole thing and call it quits. After a thorough evaluation, I took the plunge and decided that instead of buying the business I would instead offer to take over the couple's lease. It was my intention to open my very own business center. The couple agreed and I proceeded with the idea — against my lawyers' advice, I might add. Their rational was that if this business run by a couple did not make it, how would this Filipino immigrant with two young children succeed? I really had to trust my gut instincts on this one. And so I did. What I had was a burning desire to make this business center successful. Ted fully supported my vision. He didn't have a choice really — once I made up my mind, nothing could stop me and he definitely sensed that.

 Living a life of gratitude, abundance and purpose.

The couple told me that the small copy machine they had would be plenty enough for my new business, but I wasn't so sure. I saw the potential of the location. As soon as I took over their lease, I went to work negotiating with the different vendors and suppliers. I brought in two brand new, much larger copiers, and started to advertise more business-oriented services in the neighborhood. I also brought in additional office supplies. Within only six months, and to the surprise of many, my business had a positive cash flow.

This office supplies and business center mix became extremely popular with the local community. My patrons were wonderful. In the spring and summer we would often receive fresh-cut flowers and delicious fruits from our customers. Some up-and-coming authors would drop off copies of their books while musicians and actor clients would give us tickets to their concerts or theatre shows. I was overwhelmed by the positive response. Our sales kept climbing — and so did my excitement. We offered a wide variety of services to the community, and this had great impact. I was even nominated as Business Woman of the Year for Surrey. Being nominated by the local customers gave me a real boost.

Things were going so well with my business center that I believed it was time to expand. In June of 1998, I made the decision to open up another location about eight miles away. This next location was even more modern than the first. I brought in high-tech digital printers and sophisticated business equipment. I made the decision to expand

 Living a life of gratitude, abundance and purpose.

the business very fast — and this is when I stepped on the roller coaster of business ownership. In hindsight, I let my emotions rule at the time. I had a dream of the business expanding quick, but I didn't have the team in place to manage the growth.

I found myself faced with many difficult challenges. I had a high staff turnover rate, vendors who didn't follow through with their promises and, most of all, a lack of solid business systems. I could no longer handle both stores. My children and my husband needed me — and I found myself too busy to attend to them. My relationship with my very own sister (who helped a great deal at the first store) suffered terribly. Everything teetered on the brink of collapse. And, to top it all, the second store got broken into and the thieves took all of the expensive computer and copier systems, leaving us with nothing but a gigantic mess.

The insurance claim had not even been settled when the thieves struck again. The insurance company accused us of orchestrating an inside job. We were appalled. Ted, who had a full-time job of his own and occasionally helped run errands for the store, whom I believe is one of the most responsible and honest men around, was subjected to intrusive questioning. He was even forced to take a lie detector test. Since the incidents happened at night while he was out, the insurance company identified him as the main suspect. Many months went by and the case was still not settled. We had no choice but to involve legal experts. It was one of my worst business

 Living a life of gratitude, abundance and purpose.

nightmares and one of my greatest learning experiences. With the lawyers' intercession, the insurance company finally gave in to our demands and paid us what was due.

A few months thereafter, Ted was sent by his company to Germany for two months. I was left alone with two young children and two businesses to look after. A decision needed to be made — and fast! After consulting friends and business associates, we decided to take the loss, merge the two companies together and focus on just one location — the newest center.

The day Ted and I decided to close the first business center was truly painful. Seeing my initial business close was not an easy task. I felt like a failure. Did I fall short of my dreams? Did I fail my husband? In the beginning I promised him it would all work out. I asked him to trust me when we opened that first center, and now I had let him down. What could I do now? At that moment, I guess I did what I had always done to get through tough times — I grounded myself, asked for God's help and healing, and let go. It was not an easy process.

We quickly turned our focus to the second store. I thank the ever-loyal Rachel, who worked with me from day-one at the first center, for sticking with me through thick and thin. I add her to the angels of my life list. She was always there for me. She did her best to keep the business afloat and the loyal customers happy.

 Living a life of gratitude, abundance and purpose.

They loved her just as much as I did. Thankfully, many clients from the first store followed us to the second center. These customers gave me the hope and courage to let go of the past, learn from it and move on. Over the course of the next several years, the business center prospered and I was able once again to devote myself to being with my husband and watching our two lovely daughters blossom into beautiful young ladies.

A Turning Point

June 21, 2003 is a day I will never forget. Excitement was in the air. My business, now named Digi-Print Graphics Plus, was moving to its very own location. We had invested in a strata unit where we could house Digi-Print. The business was back on its feet again. There was sunshine after the storm. I always wanted to own our business building where we would no longer have to deal with landlords. Ted and Jhet would be our own landlord. Yippee! This was my tenth year in business and finally we were owners of our own location. My staff — Greg, Anna and Rachel — were all excited about our move. This would be a brand new place owned by Digi-Print Graphics. This was another dream come true for me.

We were all packed and ready for the movers to come. To celebrate our move, the staff and I ate lunch together. A huge truck finally arrived with four big burly men. There was nothing else to pack, so Anna decided to leave. Everything else was to be taken care of by the professional movers anyway. These men, Rachel, Greg and I were the only ones left at the store. The movers had just started to carry things when I noticed Rachel breathing very heavily. She didn't look good at all. One of the movers helped her to sit down immediately. I gently asked her questions but she just stared back at me with a blank expression. I did not know what was going on, but something was seriously wrong. I called 911 immediately.

Meanwhile, Rachel was no longer responding to any of us. I called Larry, Rachel's husband, and told him the ambulance was on its way. Everything was happening so fast, so very fast. Rachel was driven swiftly to the local hospital. I followed in my van. When I got to the hospital, I was shocked when I was told she had slipped into a coma. She was completely unconscious and her whole body was covered with tubes. I could not believe what was happening.

Later that night I watched helplessly as another ambulance, sirens on, took her to Vancouver General Hospital. I hardly slept at all that night. I cried so much and asked God what was happening. The first thing the next morning, her younger sister Ruth, Larry and I were on our way to the hospital. We were all very quiet and very anxious during the thirty-minute drive over there.

When we arrived at the hospital, the staff asked us to wait in a private room. Moments later a professional looking lady sadly told us that our beloved Rachel had passed away. Numb, we were escorted

Living a life of gratitude, abundance and purpose.

to the room where her warm but lifeless body lay. It was one of the hardest moments of my life. Ruth, Larry and I each took a turn saying our last goodbyes to Rachel. It was very emotional. It was the first time I had experienced such a close personal loss. We were all crying like babies. The day before, we had been packing together, exchanging friendly conversation and sharing a meal. The next day, my most loyal employee and dearest friend Rachel was gone. It was all so heartbreaking.

Rachel's sudden passing brought up many important questions for me. After all, it could so easily have been me. What did I really want to accomplish before I pass away? What legacy did I want to leave behind? Was I living my life to the fullest? Was I living life from my highest self? What is my life's purpose? Before I could really answer those questions I first had to grieve. I was now left without my right hand person. And, unfortunately, we were also still in the middle of the business move.

You can just imagine how hectic it was as friends and family tried their very best to locate where everything was supposed to go. Rachel knew where everything went. She was our production queen. Unfortunately, God decided to take her away from us and we were left to figure it out the hard way. I believe her spirit was with us during that move, though. Every now and then when we could not seem to find something, I would think about her and, like magic, the missing thing would show up. I was very blessed to have such

 Living a life of gratitude, abundance and purpose.

wonderful friends, staff and their families, and my husband and loving daughters to help with that sorrowful transition period in my life. It was a time for new discoveries and new beginnings in my life, yet again.

Chapter 10

New Beginnings

"All serious daring starts from within."
Harriet Beecher Stowe

This month of June 2005 marks the attainment of two epic milestones for me. During these thirty days, not only will I complete this very book that you are now reading, *The Tale of Juliet*, but also our family will move into our 'dream' ocean-view house overlooking the mighty Pacific Ocean this month. The ocean is from where I get my bountiful reserves of energy — along with others of God's wondrous creations, from the majestic mountains, to the shimmering stars, to the towering pines, to the absolute abundance of Mother Earth herself. But the ocean and the shoreline shall always hold a special place in my heart.

These days, whenever I walk along the seashore, I am reminded of my life as a vendor a few decades ago, as a young child selling my wares along Matabungkay Beach. This serves as the anchor for my life. No wonder I love to walk on the beach so much. Looking back at my vending days, I do not know exactly how many hundreds of times I scoured the white sands with a *bilao* over my head and a basket in my arms. But I do know that every time I passed by those

 Living a life of gratitude, abundance and purpose.

big beach houses, with people relaxing in hammocks and seemingly enjoying their lives, I somehow imagined what it would be like for me to actually one day own one of those huge homes — and now my dream has at last come true.

As I was growing up, on many occasions I experienced putting groceries back on the shelf because we did not have enough money to pay for them. During my childhood, it was obvious that we did not have the income or the time to do the things we wanted to do. I am at the point in my life now that being very poor in the past doesn't embarrass me anymore or cause personal humiliation as it did so many times when I was a child. Instead, my former social status has made me so proud of who I am today. That is why I would like to tell the people of the world this story of mine, with the desire of instilling hope and inspiration in others.

As a young girl on Matabungkay Beach, and at that tender age and situation, I could never have thought those unexpressed dreams, deeply embedded in every cell of my body, would one day come true way beyond my imaginings. God knows he has something in store for me. Such is this beautiful life of mine, I must say these words of gratitude again before this day is through: *Thank you Lord for this wonderful gift of life and for the grace of abundance I am experiencing. Thank you for my family and friends and every individual who comes along, touching and enriching my life, molding me to be who I am today.*

 Living a life of gratitude, abundance and purpose.

During the last two years I have immersed myself in multiple personal development seminars and programs throughout North America. I have flown and traveled back and forth to many different parts of Canada and the United States attending inspirational and motivational events. I have invested a great deal of time and money, and purchased many books and inspirational audio programs. I guarantee you that I have read more books in the last two years than in my entire life so far. I feel so fortunate to be able to sponsor my family members and friends to attend these seminars too. I am just blown away to experience meeting people from all walks of life with this common goal: *To be the best that we can be and to share our God-given talent with others.*

So many people have touched the essence of my being and impacted my life — I call them angels. It was during one of these 'life direction' seminars that I discovered what I really want to do for the rest of my life — I want to be an angel in the lives of others. I firmly believe I have a message for the world. This is a message of hope for the people who want to open their hearts to change, to strive to be better, to find their life's purpose and search for a meaning beyond just the accumulation of financial riches.

I want to tell people that what matters most is not the wealth you accumulate, rather the number of people you have helped while you are serving your time here on earth. We all know that money alone cannot make us happy. There is more to life than money.

 Living a life of gratitude, abundance and purpose.

Family, friends and health are all real wealth. But there is also nothing wrong with having plenty of money. Money does not really excite me on its own — what stimulates me the most is what I can share with others if I have the means with which to do it. One thing I do know for sure, from vast personal experience, is that it is better to be rich than to be poor. Why settle for less, if you can be and do so much more?

I am full of energy now, more than ever. I am so very passionate to fulfill my mission — to inspire individuals to live to their highest potential and live their life to the fullest. I want to have a positive impact on others through my story of poverty to prosperity, whether told in person, read in a book or heard on audio. These gifts of hope will be my legacy to mankind. I am having the ride of my life. I am having a marvelous time. I am not going to give up, let up or shut up from spreading my message of hope — ever! In fact, I am doing things now that I never thought I could ever do. I will keep raising my bar higher and higher.

I would like to encourage all the people of the world — young or old, black or white, down-and-out or well-to-do — to open your heart, rekindle your soul, and live up to your higher mission. You must find your purpose in life. My desire is that you will also recognize your defining moments, your turning points, and make the most of the opportunities that arise. Be inspired to take action and be the best that you possibly can. Be of service to mankind

 Living a life of gratitude, abundance and purpose.

starting from within. Let's make this world a better place. You and I, together, we can make a real difference.

Matabungkay Beach — Revisited

I have been back to this beach several times since my vending days. Let me share with you the most significant visit, just the day before I started writing this book in May 2004. I went there with my mother and father and some of my brothers and sisters and nephews and nieces — this time not with my own family, though. They stayed in Canada. God sent me on this particular trip for a higher mission.

We arrived at the beach at two o'clock in the afternoon and stayed until just after the sun had gone down. We brought a lot of food and had quite a feast. I took the time to walk back and forth along the sandy beach, barefooted, reminiscing about my past on that same white sand years and years ago. I managed to talk to several vendors and openly told them that I used to be one of them. I told them that if they have children, they must encourage them to have ambition and to never ever let go of their dreams. I explained that I am a living example that there is a better life out there.

I also stopped and chatted with the fresh-catch vendors. After I bought their prawns for our barbecue I told them my story. One lady who joined us looked familiar to me. She recognized me too.

 Living a life of gratitude, abundance and purpose.

She knew some of my classmates. That meeting with the vendors touched my life deeply. I realized how God has been so good to me and how I am truly blessed. I can still remember vividly how decades earlier, as a young child vendor, I walked on this sandy beach, back and forth with heavy loads on top of my head and in my arms, approaching each person hoping to make a sale.

These ladies carry on vending while I am enjoying an abundant life in another country. I cannot help but be emotional about it and my tears are flowing at this moment for the gratitude that is bursting forth from my heart. I can never stop thanking the Lord for the gift of abundance that manifests in my own life every day. I am so thankful that I had that humbling experience as a child, so that I now know that the power of prayer, the strength of vision, a burning desire and unwavering determination can change the course of one's life. I am now able to proudly tell the world that dreams do come true. Mine did — and yours can too.

May God bless you on your own journey through life.

 Living a life of gratitude, abundance and purpose.

ACKNOWLEDGEMENTS

There are many people to thank for their love, encouragement, guidance and inspiration to make *The Tale of Juliet* a reality.

First and foremost, to my husband, Ted, who lets me be myself and always supports me in anything I pursue, and for his contribution in putting the story pieces together, most especially our time in Yemen.

To my cheerleaders and darling daughters, Michelle and Catherine, for giving me so much joy, love and inspiration. To Catherine, also, for coming on board my editing team.

To Tom, our son-like Korean student, and his parents Jane and Patrick. Thank you for sharing your son with us and for the gift of your friendship.

To my mentor, Mark Victor Hansen, for planting the seed that I have a book in me. Mark, you're the greatest!

To Monsignor Antonio B. Unson, and his family, who helped change the course of my life. To Sister Eliza Cervantes, for giving me my name Jhet. Thank you also to her loving family. To Dr. Juanito 'Bill' B. Billiote, for his inspiration and generosity in helping me pursue higher education.

To all charitable institutions, most especially the Daughters of Charity, for giving the gift of scholarship education to less privileged children. Your mission definitely opened doors of opportunity for me.

My heartfelt gratitude to many people who have meant so much to me and who all helped bring this book to fruition. To name a few: My coach, JoAnne L. Rush, of What a Rush Productions, who initiated

 Living a life of gratitude, abundance and purpose.

the editing and believed that I have a story to tell the world. To Ruby Ann Kagaoan-Calo, who organized and edited part of the manuscript. To Susan Romero-Vidal who helped outline the chapters of my book. To Tito and Esther, my fellow guerilla marketers, who gave me a push all the way from Spain to New York. To George McMullen who is a fan of mine and a mentor too. And heartfelt gratitude to a very special mentor and friend, James Lee Valentine, who took this book to the finish line with his superb final editing, critiquing and formatting.

Thank you to many friends who helped review and critique the draft of the manuscript, including Katy Mayrs, Tami Calvert, Irene Yatco, Veronica Armstrong, Fr. Stanley Galvon and Lynn Kanuka.

Thank you to my brothers, Ohnie, Rey, Jose, Junior, Lito and sisters Aida, Cherry, Vicky, Mary Anne and their families who were my early motivation to strive for more. I especially thank those who contributed their sweet stories of our challenging and happy times together during our younger years. I am most grateful to my sister Mary Anne, who presently lives with us — she is my secretary and all-round help. I am so grateful for her undying sincere love and support. Thank you also to her fiancée Jovi and to Vicky's husband Edward for their help.

A deepest gratitude to my invaluable staff at Digi-Print Graphics Plus — Greg, Katy, Anna and Matt — for taking care of every detail of the business while I'm pursuing this new mission and passion. I love you guys. I also thank all the other employees that have since moved on with their life's calling yet have been a part of our business success. Thank you to all our customers, suppliers and fellow business colleagues for their loyal support. Without you we would not be where we are today.

Thank you to all of our friends in Canada, USA and the world over who touched, enriched and contributed to my colorful life.

 Living a life of gratitude, abundance and purpose.

For the inspirations of the many authors, seminar leaders and inspirational speakers I have met. To name a few: T. Harv Eker, Jack Canfield, James Malinchak and Brian Tracy. To other wonderful authors and speakers, from whom I learned and will continue to learn. Here are some of them: Zig Ziglar, Dr. Wayne W. Dyer, Rick Warren, Anthony Robbins, Rick Hansen, Michael E. Gerber, Robert Kiyosaki and many more for passing on their gifts of wisdom.

To all the wonderful people I have met at Peak Potentials Training, Enlightened Warrior Training Camp, Mega Speaking Empire, Mega Book Marketing University, Wizard Training Camp and many other training, speaking, writing and marketing events that I have attended. Thank you also goes to Robert G. Allen and his Protégé program support staff for making a difference in my life.

To all the wonderful people and friends I met in Holland and Yemen. Thank you for the love and support of Jan, Corry, Monique, Patrick and Lawrence.

Thank you to all the wonderful circle of friends from South Surrey, Canada, where we have made our home for seventeen years now. You know who you are and you all make my life so invigorating.

To my many good friends and wonderful people from the Philippines, may you find love, hope and inspiration and strive to make a positive difference.

And last but not the least, to you who are reading this book. Here is my life, my heart, my mind and my soul. May it touch you and give you the inspiration to hold on to your dreams and to do the things you never would have thought you could ever do. If I can do it, you can do it too, and so much more. You all have something to share with the world — find it, live it, and pass it on. I love you all.

 Living a life of gratitude, abundance and purpose.

Jhet Torcelino-van Ruyven

Jhet Torcelino-van Ruyven is an inspirational example of a person who does whatever it takes to achieve success and well being in life. Jhet came from humble beginnings. She was born in a tiny rural village in the Philippines. There was no electricity in her home and the only mode of transportation was by foot. Jhet is the second eldest of twelve children. Her family faced serious poverty throughout her childhood. In fact, from a very young age and throughout high school, Jhet helped her parents feed her brothers and sisters by vending in the villages surrounding her home. Despite growing up in an environment laden with challenge and adversity, Jhet always believed in her own potential.

Shortly after graduating from high school, Jhet was blessed by the kindness of a priest. This man helped her enroll in an exclusive school for girls. In exchange for her tuition, food and accommodation, Jhet had to clean offices, do laundry and wash dishes. At the age of eighteen she finished a medical secretarial course and was able to secure a good job in a hospital. Jhet's consistent hard work and dedication to excellence turned heads and Jhet found herself consistently promoted.

In 1984, Jhet left the Philippines to work in Yemen Arab Republic. It was in Yemen that she met the Dutch man who would become her husband. In addition to this happy occurrence, Jhet had other amazing experiences in Yemen. While volunteering for the Sisters of Charity, Jhet had the privilege of meeting Mother Teresa. Shortly thereafter, Jhet began the next chapter of her incredible life. In 1988, the newly-married Jhet and her husband immigrated to Canada.

 Living a life of gratitude, abundance and purpose.

Within two months of the young couple's arrival in Canada, Jhet was expecting her first daughter. It was then that she decided to start a home-based business. Four years later, raising two young children, she decided to go to work full-time. Once again, Jhet would prove her strong-willed determination and effective goal-setting strategies. Through her amazing sales, Jhet earned every all-expenses-paid incentive trip offered by her company — including jaunts to the Caribbean and San Diego.

In 1994 Jhet demonstrated her entrepreneurial spirit again and started her own business. Three years later, she expanded this and opened Digi-Print Graphics Plus — a successful digital printing and graphic design company. Despite many hardships, Jhet continued to persevere and the business continued to flourish. In 1996, Jhet Torcelino-van Ruyven was nominated locally as Business Woman of the Year.

In the year 2003, Jhet faced a personal tragedy that prompted her to take stock of her life. This traumatic event forced Jhet to re-examine her journey from poverty to abundance. Jhet decided she needed to show true gratitude for her good fortune. Since then, Jhet has been putting plans in place that will help her accomplish her newly defined life mission — *to inspire people to reach their full potential.* Through her story, she is doing her best to pass on a message of courage, hope and determination. Jhet Torcelino-van Ruyven is a wonderful example of the power of the human spirit. Spend a moment in her presence, and be inspired by her remarkable tale.

 Living a life of gratitude, abundance and purpose.

A Special Request From Jhet

My heartfelt thank you goes out to you for taking the precious time to read *The Tale Of Juliet*. I sincerely wish you success and happiness in life. May you find what you are looking for. Remember it all starts with a dream, but only you can make it happen for you.

If you have enjoyed this book, or if it has positively impacted your life, I would love to hear from you. Let me know of your successes, your worthy ideals, your life changing experiences and your goals.

My own goal is to get this message of *The Tale Of Juliet* to millions of people all over the world. I believe that nothing is impossible. Together we can make it happen. So, let's plant the seed of hope, inspiration and action in as many people as we can.

My mission is to pay it forward, to inspire and motivate people to live up to their highest potential. *The Tale Of Juliet* is my life, my heart and my soul. If you know of someone or any organization that can benefit from this amazing journey please pass it on.

To use *The Tale Of Juliet* for fundraising campaigns or any worthy causes, we will be delighted to assist you. And if you require additional copies of this book or wish to place a bulk order, just ask me:

jhet@thetaleofjuliet.com

Note: I am available for speaking engagements throughout North America and worldwide to help inspire all people with hope and desire.

 Living a life of gratitude, abundance and purpose.